THE DICTIONARY OF WOKE

DR KEVIN DONNELLY

HOW ORWELLIAN LANGUAGE CONTROL AND GROUP THINK ARE DESTROYING WESTERN SOCIETIES

WP

Published by Wilkinson Publishing Pty Ltd
ACN 006 042 173
Level 6, 174 Collins Street, Melbourne, VIC 3000
Ph: +61 3 9654 5446
enquiries@wilkinsonpublishing.com.au
www.wilkinsonpublishing.com.au

WilkinsonPublishing
wilkinsonpublishinghouse
WPBooks

This is an updated and revised edition of Kevin Donnelly's *A Politically Correct Dictionary and Guide* (2019).
Reprinted 2022

ISBN: 9781922810090
eBook ISBN: 9781922810205
A catalogue record for this book is available from the National Library of Australia.

Cover and internal design by Ben Davis.

Printed and bound in Australia by Griffin Press

CONTENTS

FOREWORD

As a middle-aged, follicularly-challenged, heterosexual Australian, assigned male at birth, who has often expressed politically right-of-centre views and is comfortable in my own skin, I have come to accept the harsh reality that my opinion is worthless. The woke have a shorthand term to describe and dismiss the likes of me – RWNJ (Right Wing Nut Job).

Yes, even though my most radical political positions are to support a constitutionally enshrined voice to parliament for Indigenous Australians and demand a truly national approach to the administration and umpiring of the AFL, my mainstream views see me branded a nut job. No wonder these people have no understanding of the voting public – their neighbours.

That is the thing about the compassionistas, despite virtue-signalling on a range of humanitarian issues, displaying sanctimony, advocating inclusivity, and championing the Love Media, they turn out to be deeply intolerant. Ostensibly, the reason they torture phraseology and butcher language is to help make everyone feel included, but in practice it is a device to rail against the established order and demonise opponents.

They proclaim support for gender equity and religious and racial tolerance but they condemn and attack Christians, people with white skin and women who are not radical feminists. Woe betide a middle-aged, white, heteronormative male entering any debate; it is not the merits of the argument that matter so much as the politically-correct ranking of the advocate's perceived or claimed identity.

The timeless words of Martin Luther King Junior seem to have become, well, dated – they are lost on this lot. Rather than ignoring the colour of someone's skin and judging them by the content of their character, these people see identity first and often exclusively. King might as well have stood at the Washington monument and proclaimed that he had a dream to live in a land where people would overlook the character of his children and judge them by the colour of their skin, their sexual preference, gender identity and wokeness.

What we are seeing is sociological regression, a tragic U-turn from King's central message, with language its key tool.

Kevin Donnelly has done us all a great service by compiling and revising this dictionary. It is a guide to the contemporary insanity, a reference point for how language is being weaponised, and a crucial documentation of the decline of intellectual integrity as we mourn what some of us like to refer to as common sense.

Even the word "mate" – central to our nation's character because of the phlegmatic way it encapsulates our predisposition towards inclusion and egalitarianism – has become a target of the woke. Government ministers in New South Wales received Respect at Work training and were told not to use the word – apparently the familiarity it infers with some can exclude others.

The inanity of such thinking, if we can call it that, is infuriating enough. But to think about how it undermines our national character, ruins a perfectly wonderful evolution of language and culture, and creates conditions for people to second guess even their most casual conversations, it is disheartening and disturbing.

Perhaps someone soon will take offence at the word "kangaroo" as an Anglicisation of one particular indigenous language to the exclusion of others. Anything could happen.

Certainly, a heterosexual woman ought not refer to her "husband" nor he refer to his "wife" – that could lead to seriously woke tut-tutting about gendered and proprietorial language. But if a woman happens to be married to a woman, or there is a male couple, then "wife" and "husband" suddenly become terms to be trumpeted. Go figure.

The point is that there is no figuring to be done. This stuff is beyond logical explanation, it is about emotional manipulation and cultural dislocation.

In these pages Donnelly methodically explains to us real phenomenon such as "lawfare" or "dead naming" in a contemporaneous diary of our descent into wokeness. He includes "Islamophobia" – a kind of reverse-victim invention that is so insidious it has generated hostility, division and even violence on both sides of the religious divide.

The author includes an entry for LGBTIQ+ which is very instructive. It translates as lesbian, gay, bisexual, transgender, intersex and queer, with the plus sign denoting any other of our apparently infinite gender or sexual preferences. But as if to prove that this sphere is the particle accelerator of culture and language, the very next entry is LGBTQA+ in which intersex has disappeared and asexual has been added, but even still, the catch-all plus sign lingers.

Presumably the intersex community is now covered by the plus sign, in fact this whole configuration should be covered by the plus sign alone, but that would provide a confusing interface between language and maths. Perhaps the tedium will soon have us all congregating under the letter A for asexual.

Whatever letters he chooses to place before or after his name, Kevin Donnelly is an author, educationalist, columnist and lexicographer who sees what we all see, thinks what we all think and has the diligence and courage to curate it. He is clearly awake to what is going on – which is, of course, the quality from which the word woke derives. Ironically, that means Donnelly must truly be woke, but in a way that benefits us all.

Chris Kenny
Host of The Kenny Report – Sky News
Associate Editor (National Affairs) – *The Australian*

INTRODUCTION

After reading *The Official Politically Correct Dictionary and Handbook* in the early 1990s I never realised how infectious, dangerous and widespread political correctness would become. Most of the examples back then were humorous and appeared far-fetched with examples like "vertically challenged" instead of small and "chemically inconvenienced" for being drunk.

Fast forward to more recent times and it's obvious cultural-left language control and group think now dominate the Western world. Whether the United Kingdom, Europe, the United States of America, Canada, Australia or New Zealand, not a week goes by without yet another example of books being banned, ideas being censored, the past being rewritten, statues being demolished and authors and academics being vilified and publicly shamed.

Now rebadged as being "woke" political correctness represents an existential threat to Western societies including concepts like rationality and reason, religious freedom and freedom of expression. We have entered an Orwellian world like 1984 where Big Brother and the Party control how citizens think and where anyone who questions the thought police is victimised, punished and silenced.

For years praised as an accomplished and successful author JK Rowling is now condemned as transphobic for arguing against radical transgender theory. In her resignation letter Bari Weiss, an accomplished writer for The New York Times, describes how she was bullied and isolated because of committing what she terms "Wrongthink". For simply arguing for balance and objectivity in how issues and events were reported Weiss was treated as an outcast. Such is the destructive nature of what he terms the "appalling ideology of Diversity, Inclusion and Equity" that Jordan Peterson resigned from his academic position at the University of Toronto. As argued by non-binary radical feminist Camille Paglia, such is the debilitating and destructive nature of political correctness, "We are plunged once again into an ethical chaos where intolerance masquerades as tolerance and where individual liberty is crushed by the tyranny of the group".

In schools and universities, as a result of neo-Marxist inspired critical race and post-colonial theories, students are taught Western societies are inherently racist, there is nothing beneficial about Western civilisation and, if they are white, told they must atone for past crimes committed against People of Colour (POC) including exploitation, cruelty, slavery, dispossession and genocide.

Such is the insidious and dangerous impact of critical race theory on schools American parents are orchestrating campaigns and state governments are now legislating to ensure a balanced and impartial curriculum. Commentators agree one of the reasons republican Glenn Youngkin is now Governor of Virginia is because of his strident opposition to schools indoctrinating students with CRT. The United Kingdom's Secretary of State for Education, Nadhim Zahawi, has promised to issue guidelines designed to ensure teachers "make a balanced presentation of opposing views on political issues" on the basis "education (is) not indoctrination". Zahawi's comments follow last year's parliamentary committee report arguing against woke terms like "white privilege" on the basis the expression leads to the neglect of already disadvantaged white, working-class students.

In Australia, the neo-Marxist inspired gender fluidity program Safe Schools, funded by state, territory and commonwealth governments, tells primary and secondary school students boys can be girls and girls can be boys. Explicit in the program is the belief there is nothing normal or preferential about being a boy or a girl and that those who disagree are guilty of homophobia, transphobia and cis-normativity. One resource even suggests parents need not be told if their child wants to undergo gender transition and nowhere in the program is there any recognition of the dangers of puberty blockers and undergoing life changing surgery.

A recent discussion paper informing government guidelines for kindergartens and preschools argues gender is fluid and binary and young children can self-identify anywhere on the LGBTIQ+ spectrum as there is nothing normal about being a boy or a girl. To suggest gender and sexuality are binary is to be guilty of heteronormativity and cis-genderism.

Such is the power and dominance of radical gender theory that the principal of a Christian school in Brisbane, Queensland was pressured to resign for simply stating it's a biological fact supported by the word of God that children are born either female or male. In England radical gender theory is part of the school curriculum and faith-based schools are punished by the school inspection body (Ofsted) if they fail to conform. Proven by events in Canada parents are also punished if they dare to question the state's right to impose theories about gender and sexuality that contradict what they, as parents, see as the truth.

The Australian Respectful Relationships program provides yet another example of how the cultural-left has infiltrated and taken control of the school curriculum. The program gives the impression women are the only victims of domestic violence, ignoring men are also affected, and implies all men are misogynist towards women. Boys in primary and secondary schools are made to feel guilty and nowhere is there any mention of the benefits of virtuous masculinity.

As argued by Camille Paglia in 'Are men obsolete?', third wave feminists are guilty of "stereotyping, belittling or demonizing men" ignoring the reality there is much to praise about masculinity and that men also suffer disadvantage.

Bettina Arndt, the Australian author of #MenToo, puts a similar argument when writing how woke, feminist ideology discriminates against men. Examples include "battles in the family court, false abuse accusations, paternity fraud, education pitched in favour of girls, unequal health funding, the distorted debate over domestic violence".

Such is the power of woke ideology that much valued and appreciated literary works are regularly condemned and cancelled. Examples include Huckleberry Finn (using the word nigger), To Kill a Mockingbird (promoting white saviour complex), Moby Dick (killing whales) and Lord of the Flies (all the characters are white, male and privileged). Children's stories are not immune to wokeism and cancel culture. Victims include Thomas the Tank Engine (enforcing capitalist hierarchies), Little Black Sambo (racism), Sleeping Beauty (heteronormativity and non-consensual sex) and Enid Blyton's The Faraway Tree (no assertive roles for girls).

Much valued literary works published with the best of intentions are also targeted by the woke thought police. In England, the University of Leicester has decided to cancel such literary classics as The Canterbury Tales, Beowulf and Le Morte D'Arthur in order to de-colonise the curriculum and present students with texts that properly reflect "ethnicity, sexuality and diversity" characterising contemporary society.

Another example of censorship involves Kate Clanchy who, after being celebrated for collecting and publishing a poetry anthology written by disadvantaged students, was condemned for stereotyping her students and culturally appropriating their works. Such were the criticisms the author's publisher Pan McMillian reverted the rights to her books and stopped their distribution. Clanchy was cancelled even though many of her former students publicly defended her and argued she was primarily responsible for empowering them to write poetry.

Nothing is immune for the cultural-left's thought police with even food and beverages targeted. The list includes American and Australian food brands like Coon Cheese, Redskins, Aunt Jemima, Dixie beer and Eskimo Pie being condemned for cultural appropriation and reinforcing unconscious bias. Apparently, any child allowed to eat Coon Cheese or slurp an Eskimo Pie on a hot summer day is infected with racism and will grow up xenophobic and guilty of white supremacism.

To cure Western societies of racism all that must be done is rebrand and market products now considered politically incorrect and offensive. Ignored is such misplaced tokenism does nothing to redress the very real disadvantage often suffered by people of colour. Instead of virtue signalling and acting morally superior a much better idea is to address what causes disadvantage and to empower those at risk to better their lives.

While justified as a request for greater civility and the avoidance of unjustified discrimination over the last 40 years political correctness has morphed into an Orwellian nightmare of distorted language and mind control.

George Orwell writes "But if thought corrupts language, language can also corrupt thought" and there is no doubt we are now living in a world where reason and rationality no longer prevail and where words, phrases and concepts have been weaponised by the cultural-left in its campaign to impose its ideological agenda.

Best illustrated by the slogan "War Is Peace, Freedom Is Slavery, Ignorance is Strength", the strategy is to force citizens to accept two or more conflicting concepts, thus, ensuring compliance by determining how people conceptualise and think. Orwell writes doublethink involves the ability "...to hold simultaneously two opinions which cancelled out, knowing them to be contradictory and believing in both of them, to use logic against logic".

Such is the bizarre and irrational world of woke babies are no longer born as girls or boys, rather they are assigned a gender at birth with some parents waiting months before they decide where their newborn infant sits on the LGBTIQ+ spectrum. In maternity hospitals breast feeding is described as chest feeding and mothers renamed birthing parents and fathers as non-gestational persons. Woke language is also used as a weapon to vilify and attack those who refuse to conform or who dare to question what has become the new orthodoxy.

Men arguing not all males are sexual predators and that women should be aware of the dangers involved in walking alone through a deserted, dark park at 3.00am in the morning, are condemned as misogynist and sexist. Any who suggest not all cultures are equal and that new arrivals should make some attempt to assimilate are attacked as racist and xenophobic. To argue it is wrong schools and universities always portray Western civilisation as classist, sexist, homophobic, racist and guilty of oppressing the other is guilty of white supremacism. One only has to follow debates on social media sites like Twitter where primitive group think and hysteria prevail to realise raw emotion has long since replaced civility, rationality and reason. In this brave new world of cultural-left mind control Descartes's maxim 'I think, therefore I am' is replaced by 'I feel, therefore I am right'.

While a recent phenomenon, the origins of political correctness and wokeness can be traced to Germany's Frankfurt School established in the mid-1920s and before that to the work of the German philosopher Friedrich Nietzsche considered by many as the father of nihilism. The Frankfurt School championed critical theory and cultural Marxism and the academics involved included

Max Horkheimer, Theodor Adorno, Erich Fromm, Herbert Marcuse, and Walter Benjamin. All advocated a radically new and all-encompassing interpretation of classical Marxist thought, in part, due to the realisation the proletarian revolution would never occur in the West. Instead of expecting capitalism to decline because of its inherent contradictions and the course of history they argued for a liberating and emancipatory form of radical change directed at the cultural foundations of Western societies.

As described by the Italian academic Augusto Del Noce in his essay 'Authority versus Power' published in The Crisis of Modernity:

> Their revolutionary stance is a radical affirmation of the transition "from the reign of necessity to the reign of freedom," understood in the strongest sense. Thus, the disappearance of authority must be viewed as the end point of progressive thought, which, in fact, presents itself as a process of liberation from authority, theological or human, transcendent or empirical...

The '60s sexual liberation movement, the cultural-left's preoccupation with radical gender theory, where human biology is negated, the argument knowledge is a social construct based on power relationships and there are no absolute truths can all be traced to the Frankfurt School.

Religion, especially Christianity, has been an especial target of cultural Marxism drawing on Antonio Gramsci's description of socialism as the "religion destined to kill Christianity". The fact any who disagree with or fail to conform to woke ideology are immediately attacked and silenced is also attributable to the totalitarian nature of cultural Marxism and the belief civility, impartiality and morality must be rejected in the battle to overturn capitalism and herald a man-made utopia on this earth.

Like Lenin's statement "Morality is whatever serves the success of the proletarian revolution" and drawing on Marcuse's essay 'Repressive Tolerance' woke activists go to any lengths to force their ideology on people and silence any opposition.

The cultural revolution of the '60s, when all forms of authority were challenged and undermined and where a range of radical, liberating philosophies, including deconstructionism, postmodernism and feminist, gender and postcolonial theories arose also underpins political correctness and wokeism. As a result, literary classics are deconstructed and analysed in terms of gender, ethnicity and class, the history of Western civilisation is characterised by white supremacism, imperialism and exploitation and Western societies like England, America and Australia are riven with structural sexism, homophobia, transphobia, classism and racism.

Such is the power and dominance of cultural-left ideology and the threat it represents to Western civilisation the English cultural critic and public intellectual Roger Scruton writes in Conservatism, "Understanding political correctness and finding ways to combat it have therefore become prominent among conservative causes" and, as a result, the culture wars are "central to their sense of what they are fighting for and why". Scruton also argues conservatives, in particular, are duty bound to "rediscover what we are and what we stand for, and having rediscovered it, be prepared to fight for it. That is now, as it has ever been, the conservative message. And what we stand for is a religious as much as a political inheritance".

That such a battle needs to be engaged is made even more crucial at a time of international uncertainty and conflict illustrated by Putin's invasion of the Ukraine and Xi Jinping's campaign to achieve global hegemony. If ever there was a time for the West to be confident and assertive and convinced of its own validity and worth, then this is it.

WOKE WORDS AND EXPRESSIONS

1. **Ableism.** An unwarranted and unjustified prejudice against those who are disabled committed by able bodied people.

2. **Ableist language**. Sara Nović, in 'The harmful ableist language you unknowingly use' on the BBC website Equality Matters, argues ableist expressions and words like "turn a blind eye", "falling on deaf ears" and making a "dumb" choice represent micro-assaults directed against disabled people. Nović writes expressions like these can do real, lasting harm to the people whom these words and phrases undermine – and even the people who use them in daily conversation, too. The Washington Inclusive Language Guide also warns against using expressions like "blind to the truth" and "blind spot".

3. **Aboriginal and Torres Strait Islander science.** The Australian Curriculum Assessment and Reporting Authority (ACARA) argues indigenous science must be taught at all year levels in science classes. The justification for putting indigenous science on the same footing as Western science is because teachers need to "provide a more culturally responsive curriculum".

Schools are told "indigenous history, culture, knowledge and understanding can be incorporated into teaching core scientific concepts" and Australia's Indigenous peoples "have explored the many wonders of our continent for millennia" and "through their rich enduring legacy, we can inspire the same instinct to explore in our students today". Critics of putting indigenous science on the same footing as Western science are described as promoting a "racist diatribe" that ignores indigenous peoples "lived here before 'Western enlightenment' arrived and started raping and killing them". The Aboriginal activist Warren Mundine, while accepting the need to teach about indigenous history and culture, argues differently when saying science is science regardless of ethnicity or race. He argues "What is indigenous physics? Physics is physics. If we are to compete in the job market we must learn technology and engineering, we need to be taught subjects properly". The move to put indigenous science in the curriculum is part of the cultural-left's global campaign to decolonise the curriculum by ridding it of Eurocentrism and whiteness.

4. **Absorgender.** LGBTIQ+ defines absorgender "as a gender in which one absorbs the genders of the people around them. As one is around more people more genders are added to the genders one feels, even after the people leave one still feels their gender. These genders remain until one reaches a 'maximum', at which point they become a blank slate, and revert to a single 'base' gender. This base gender can be any gender, including agender. For some people this 'base' gender may be different each time". Examples include absorboy, absorgirl and absorbinary. See *The Conservative Woman's* essay titled 'Gender obsession seizes our legal watchdog' written by Caroline Ffiske for an argument why gender ideology is a threat to freedom of speech.

5. **Affinity Bias.** The natural inclination to prefer socialising and working with similar types of people, according to woke activists pushing identity politics and victimhood, is an example of affinity bias. Especially guilty are Eurocentric, misogynist, homophobic males who refuse to mix with those categorised as the "other". Such unwoke people should never be allowed in the workplace or invited to social events as their views are offensive and unacceptable.

6. **Ageism.** The belief that those old enough to remember black and white TVs, red telephone boxes, garage pump attendants and Xerox machines are obsolete and of little value. The Sydney academic Teena Clerke was a victim

of ageism when a student complained on an online survey seeking feedback from students "This woman is so old her views are redundant. She hasn't designed anything since the internet. Why do we need her?" Older people, otherwise known as the chronologically challenged, are digitally inept and adhere to obsolete behaviour including civility, good manners, not eating in public and expecting children to be well behaved and respect adults.

7. **Agitprop.** The Oxford Dictionary defines agitprop as "political (originally communist) propaganda, especially in art or literature". The expression is used more widely now to refer to any attempt, usually by the cultural-left, to use the media to circulate propaganda and fake news to influence social and political debates. President Trump regularly criticises the American liberal-left media for being guilty of fake news and after a meeting with President Putin tweeted "The Summit with Russia was a great success, except with the real enemy of the people, the Fake News Media".

8. **Alcoholic.** Describing somebody as an alcoholic is demeaning and offensive as such individuals are often the victims of events beyond their control caused by an oppressive society. More politically correct alternatives include "substance abuse survivor" and "chemically inconvenienced individual".

9. **Alt-right.** Short for alternative right and the expression is used to describe extreme right-wing organisations and individuals who reject conservatism and espouse a racist, white supremacist ideology.

10. **Anchor baby.** A term originating in America used to describe babies born to illegal immigrants that enable the parents to have a better chance of claiming citizenship and being allowed to resettle. After the Australian Home Affairs Minister Peter Dutton used the expression, he was attacked in the twittersphere by Noel Miller as follows "Anchor baby is a racist term used in the US by anti-immigration activists, demonising children of non-citizen adults, who allegedly use their kids who were born in the US to gain citizenship".

11. **Andorcentrism.** Defined as privileging men by treating them as dominant and excluding women and LGBTIQ+ people. For example, the expression "he's a man's man" is phallocentric as it suggests that manliness in boys and men is an admirable quality, when second and third wave feminists argue they should be more like women. The politically correct alternative to "he's a man's man" is "zie is a non-gendered individual's intersex person who should be celebrated in a non-binary way".

12. **Animals.** Otherwise known as "non-human sentient creatures" as the description "animals" suggests an inferior status leading to exploitation and cruelty. *The Journal of Animal Ethics*, edited by Reverend Professor Andrew Linzey, argues "wild animals" is unacceptable as it suggests an uncivilised, unrestrained and barbarous existence.

13. **Art washing.** Refers to organisations, companies and governments financially supporting artists, musicians, dancers, artistic events and festivals in order to legitimise and cloak actions defined by the woke brigade as unacceptable. The organisers of the 2022 Sydney Festival were accused of art washing after it was discovered one of the acts had received funding from the Israeli embassy.

14. **Australia Day.** Aboriginal activists argue Australia Day is a "day of mourning and a day of shame" and describe the arrival of the First Fleet as an invasion. An invasion, according to Dr Hannah McGlade a Senior Indigenous Research Fellow at Curtin University, leading to the "genocide" of Australia's Indigenous people. Those celebrating the arrival of the First Fleet and the establishment of a British penal colony are condemned as Eurocentric and guilty of white supremacism. The revised Australian national curriculum released mid-2021 describes the arrival of the First Fleet as "genocide".

15. **Bald.** A description once used to describe those, usually men, with no hair. Politically correct alternatives include "follicularly challenged" and "hair disadvantaged".

16. **BAME.** A politically correct acronym referring to those living in the UK who are black, Asian, minority ethnic. Used on the basis that descriptions such as English or British reinforce white privilege and deny the identity of those who are categorised and mis-treated as the "Other".

17. **BC/AD.** Traditional Christian terms once used to describe the period before and after the birth of Christ with BC referring to the period before the birth of Christ and AD coming from the Latin Anno Domini referring to "in the year of the Lord". Such terms privilege Christianity as a religion and are offensive in our diverse, multi-faith, multicultural society; a society that celebrates diversity and difference and where all cultures and religions are equal (except for Christianity). The politically correct alternatives are BCE (Before the Common Era) and CE (Common Era).

18. **Bed wetters.** Originating in America the expression is used in Australia to describe those centre-left parliamentary members of the Liberal Party who betrayed the then Prime Minister Tony Abbott by replacing him with Malcolm Turnbull. They argued Abbott was too conservative and that as Turnbull was seen as progressive in areas like climate change, same-sex marriage and multiculturalism he would

be more electorally appealing. In the 2016 Commonwealth election the Turnbull government was nearly defeated and such were Turnbull's failures and inability to lead he was replaced as Prime Minister by Scott Morrison in 2018.

19. **Bierasure.** The Monash University Diversity and Inclusion Glossary defines bierasure as "questioning or denying the existence or legitimacy of bisexuality (either in general or in regard to an individual)".

20. **Binary.** Binary concepts like male/female, heterosexual/homosexual, civilised/primitive, black/white are politically incorrect as they reinforce and reproduce an inequitable system of exploitation and marginalisation associated with Western, capitalist power structures. For example, to describe pre-1788 Aboriginal tribes as primitive because they had not invented the wheel and there were no printing presses, roads, buildings, steam engines or clearly defined and sophisticated forms of law and government is to be guilty of imposing a Eurocentric concept employed to justify the invasion. The binary description male/female is also offensive as it reinforces the belief that just because approximately 98% of Australians self-identify as women and men that heterosexuality is the norm.

21. **Biological essentialism.** Research proving a significant number of the differences between men and women are

determined by nature, as girls at birth have XX chromosomes while boys have XY, is described by radical feminists as "biological determinism" imposed by a patriarchal, oppressive society. Second and third wave feminists prefer to believe that gender and sexuality are social constructs as then all they must do in order to change society is to mandate people's beliefs and attitudes and all will be well.

22. **Biphobia.** An unwarranted and irrational prejudice against those who are bisexual.

23. **BIPOC.** In America and Australia the acronym refers to members of black, indigenous and people of colour communities. Similar to the acronym BAME (standing for Black, Asian and Minority Ethnic) widespread in the UK, the description embraces identity politics and victimhood as Western societies are guilty of structural racism, unconscious bias and riven with white supremacism. Five art critics working for the *Sydney Morning Herald* and *The Age* resigned soon after being employed because of their "whiteness". They argued it was racist to deny BIPOC people employment and it was no longer acceptable to only have "one voice in the room". One of the critics Tirney Miekus was quoted in *The Daily Telegraph* arguing the situation was "completely appalling and shameful" and part of her salary should be used "to publish arts pieces by black, indigenous, people of colour writers". (See also POC.)

24. **Birthing parent.** The *Gender Inclusive Handbook* prepared by the Australian National University Gender Institute and the Centre for Learning and Teaching suggests when discussing childbirth to use the terms "gestational" or "birthing" parent rather than "mother", and the terms "nongestational" or "nonbirthing" parent rather than "father". While biology determines mothers give birth, lactate and breastfeed the handbook argues traditional descriptions are heteronormative and guilty of offending those "who do not identify with gender-binaries".

25. **Blackfishing.** CNN Entertainment's Faith Karima writes "Blackfishing is when White public figures, influencers and the like do everything in their power to appear Black". Examples include tanning their skin, changing their hairstyle and clothing to suggest blackness.

26. **Blacking up/Black facing.** An example of cultural appropriation where white people blacken their faces. While common on screen and stage in the past blacking up is now considered demeaning and offensive to people of colour. An example of blacking up includes the 1964 film *Mary Poppins* when she appears on the roof with her face covered in soot and dancing with chimney sweeps. The characters are described as "Hottentots" and in *The New York Times* Daniel Pollack-Pelzer argues "These aren't really black Africans; they're grinning white dancers in blackface. It's a parody of

black menace; it's even posted on a white nationalist website as evidence of the film's racial hierarchy".

27. **Blacktivist.** Refers to those advocating the rights of Aboriginal and Torres Strait Islander people against a government that is Eurocentric, oppressive and responsible for the genocide, dispossession and theft that has occurred since the arrival of the First Fleet. The fact Indigenous Australians have the same political and legal rights as white Australians, that decisions like Mabo guarantee indigenous ownership of land and that billions are spent every year to support the Aborigine and Torres Strait Islander self-serving industry is ignored.

28. **Blind leading the blind.** Visually impaired people consider this expression offensive as it mistakenly suggests their condition denotes a weakness or inability to see things clearly. The correct expression is "the sight impaired leading the visually challenged".

29. **Body shaming.** Defined as abusing and shaming people whose body shapes do not conform to the white, patriarchal, capitalist, marketing stereotype. When the British TV personality Jameela Jamil was confronted by a man commenting about her appearance she answered "Never walk up to someone and tell them how much better they could look. You're not being nice, you're shaming

them for the way they currently look. You're also being extremely weird".

30. **Bodies with vaginas.** The British journal *Lancet* was criticised in 2021 for a front cover that included the statement "Historically, the anatomy and physiology of bodies with vaginas have been neglected". The journal's editor was criticised for using the description "bodies with vaginas" instead of women as it both demeaned and commodified what it meant to be a woman.

31. **Bodily autonomy.** As reported by the *Australian*'s Helen Trinca (*The Australian,* Sunday 21 March 2021), the Sydney University academic Penny Russell argues men use the strategy of denying women bodily autonomy to enforce their domination and control. Russell argues "The use of women's bodies to police their conduct in public and to police their access to power has been very constant, and it has always been in different ways a focus for feminists".

32. **Boomerang wings.** As reported by the Australian journalist Susie O'Brien in *The Herald Sun* (20 March 2021) Woolworths was pressured to rename this chicken cut as some customers considered it racist and an example of cultural appropriation. A spokesman from Woolworths is reported as saying "We've reviewed the feedback and decided it's appropriate to change the description of this particular cut to 'V wings'". Ignored is the fact that the

imperialist, racist British war time prime minister Winston Churchill often used the "V" sign as a sign of white solidarity during the London blitz.

33. **Bots.** A term used by internet game players to denigrate other players by suggesting they play like non-human, AI software. As in "you make such dumb decisions you must be a Bot".

34. **Call out culture.** In October 2019 during an interview given at the Obama Foundation President Obama warned against the growing tendency, especially via the internet and social networking sites, of those who are woke to immediately condemn any holding opposing beliefs and views. When discussing "call out culture" the former President of the United States argues "This idea of purity and you're never compromised and you're always politically 'woke' and all that stuff... You should get over that quickly. The world is messy; there are ambiguities... People who do really good stuff have flaws. People who you are fighting may love their kids and share certain things with you."

35. **Cancel culture.** Anyone who opposes or is critical of political correctness faces the danger of being attacked and silenced and denied the right to freedom of expression and open debate. Public intellectuals, media commentators and famous sportsmen and sportswomen are especially vulnerable to being cancelled as proven by the example of Australia's

Bettina Arndt and Germaine Greer. Both have been denied permission to speak on university campuses because of their anti-PC views about gender and sexuality. Of concern is that universities no longer protect academic freedom as proven by the increasing number of academics intimidated and criticised for daring to question the prevailing cultural-left orthodoxy.

In *Time* magazine's 21 November 2019 issue Sara Hagi puts a counter-argument suggesting "cancel culture" is used as a "catch-all for when people in power face consequences for their actions or receive any type of criticism, something that they're not used to". Hagia argues because of the prevalence of social media "racist, sexist, and bigoted behaviour or remarks don't fly like they used to" and it's now more common for such behaviour to be condemned and for those responsible made to suffer. (See also no platforming.)

36. **Captain Cook.** Captain Cook is a DWEM (dead, white, European male). By claiming what is now the east coast of Australia for Britain in 1770 Cook shares responsibility for the white invasion and the genocide of Australia's Indigenous peoples. In fact, there was no genocide. Most Aborigines who died were victims of new diseases. Stan Grant, a commentator on the Australian Broadcasting Commission, when discussing Cook's statue in Sydney's Hyde Park argues "Yet this statue speaks to emptiness, it speaks to our invisibility; it says that nothing truly mattered,

nothing truly counted until a white sailor first walked on these shores. The statue speaks still to terra nullius and the violent rupture of Aboriginal society and a legacy of pain and suffering that endures today".

37. **Casual sexism.** Refers to the way patriarchal society reinforces gender stereotyping in ways that might not always be immediately obvious. Children's books, for example, often present boys in physically assertive roles while female characters are portrayed as feminine and passive. In late 2019 a British retailer was condemned for selling colouring books titled *Brave knights colouring book for boys* while the girl's version was titled *My pretty princess colouring book*. (See also unconscious bias.)

38. **Catfishing.** Described by Caroline Overington in *The Australian* newspaper as "the process of creating a fake persona online to dupe somebody into making a romantic attachment".

39. **Change adaptors.** According to a report in Melbourne's *The Age* (26 March 2019) the principal of Melbourne's Siena College argues librarians are obsolete. Siena College now has what are described as change adaptors who "host discussions with students and teach 'soft skills' such as ethical and creative thinking". The principal also argues "If you think about it you don't need to go to the library to do

research and you don't need a librarian to talk to you about interesting literature or books".

40. **Chestmilk.** A non-binary, gender-neutral description instead of breastmilk. Using the description breastmilk is wrong as it privileges and reinforces the heteronormative concept that only those assigned female at birth are able to lactate and feed their child.

41. **Christopher Columbus.** Like Captain Cook who charted the eastern coast of Australia, Columbus who discovered America, is now decidedly politically incorrect and considered yet another DWEM. Los Angeles has replaced Columbus Day with Indigenous Day as contemporary America is built on the exploitation and enslavement of indigenous inhabitants who lived in harmony with the land and coexisted peacefully. Before Europeans invaded what is now America the numerous tribes that existed never engaged in warfare, stole from one another or exploited one another's territories.

42. **Christianity.** Defined as a Eurocentric, oppressive myth based on superstition and a mistaken belief in miracles and the afterlife. The father of communism Karl Marx describes religion as "the opium of the people" and the Italian Marxist Antonio Gramsci describes socialism as "the religion destined to kill Christianity". More recently, the English academic Richard Dawkins in *The God Delusion* argues "Faith can be

very, very dangerous, and deliberately to implant it into the vulnerable mind of an innocent child is a grievous wrong".

43. **Christianophobia.** Patrick Sookhdeo in *The Death of Western Christianity* argues we are living in an intolerant and oppressive "anti-Christian age". He describes Christianophobia as "a state of fear and hatred against Christianity and Christians".

44. **Christmas carols.** Used by religious adherents to indoctrinate young children with binary concepts like right and wrong, good and bad and treating others as you would have them treat you. Many schools ban Christmas carols as they privilege Christianity over other religions and faiths in Australia's multicultural, multi-faith society. In order to celebrate diversity and difference if carols are sung, they must not refer to the birth of Christ or celebrate Christmas as a religious occasion.

45. **Chronic Truth Aversion Disorder (CTAD).** Described as the inability and unwillingness of the woke to acknowledge there is truthfulness in issues and arguments where they disagree. The Australian Aboriginal activist Anthony Dillion writes CTAD "is raging through Australia's social media population", thus making it impossible to have an "intelligent debate on serious social issues, such as the rampant violence, abuse and neglect of children in remote indigenous communities".

46. **Chronologically challenged.** Otherwise known as the aged or old people. (See also ageism.)

47. **Cis-splaining.** Similar to man-splaining, where men dominate the debate and woman are ignored or treated condescendingly, cis-plaining involves heteronormative, cispeople controlling discussion and debate and ignoring the voices of transpeople.

48. **Cisgender.** Refers to those Cismen and Ciswomen who have been conditioned to be happy with the biological sex they were assigned at birth. The blogger Jeff Estevez argues that Cisgender is a capitalist inspired, oppressive concept employed to erase the fact that there are multiple genders, he argues "Colonialism and other power structures have tried really hard to erase this and enforce a strict gender binary so that there is also a strict power hierarchy".

49. **Cisnormativity.** Monash University's 'Inclusive Teaching Toolkit' describes this as assuming "that everyone is cisgender and that all people will continue to identify with the gender they were assigned at birth". Cisnormativity erases the existence of trans, queer and gender diverse people.

50. **Cissexism.** The Safe Schools 'OMG I'm Trans' booklet describes Cissexim as "The assumption that everyone is straight and Cisgender".

51. **Citizenship.** Being a citizen no longer involves supporting the country in which you were born and to which you owe allegiance, instead, as detailed in the draft of the Australian 'Civics and Citizenship' curriculum "Citizenship means different things to people at different times and depending on personal perspectives, their social situation and where they live". Citizenship involves multiple perspectives that "reflect personal, social, spatial and temporal dimensions of citizenship". As such it is wrong to deny citizenship to those Muslim Australians, like Neil Prakash, who fought with ISIS in the Middle East to establish an Islamic caliphate.

52. **Clickbait.** A text or link that tempts the user to click on the link and go to the associated site on the internet.

53. **Climate denier.** Even though the science is far from settled regarding man-made global warming, politically correct activists denounce any who disagree with the prevailing orthodoxy as climate deniers. Bjorn Lomborg who questions the causal relationship between carbon and global warming is attacked in the Twittersphere as "an idiotic moron" and someone dedicated to promoting a "neoconservative conspiracy agenda".

54. **Cocooning.** The Australian Domino's pizza company CEO Don Meij explains the dramatic increase in home delivery sales by what he describes as "cocooning" – a situation where "Eating in the home is a greater trend, binge watching with

Netflix, that is a global trend in food delivery and the fastest growth part of our business is delivered food and that is not exclusive to Australia, I can point to Europe as well" (*The Australian*, 19 February 2020).

55. **Coercive secularism.** According to Jibran Khan, a Fellow at the United Kingdom's National Review Institute, coercive secularism involves undermining and restricting the right of religious bodies and organisations to adhere to their faith. Khan gives the example of faith-based schools being reprimanded for not teaching the government mandated view about gender and sexual fluidity and diversity.

56. **Cognitive dissonance.** Refers to the ability to hold two or more contradictory thoughts or beliefs at the one time and not to understand they are in opposition. Described by George Orwell as "Doublethink" involving the "power of holding two contradictory beliefs in one's mind simultaneously and accepting both of them". An example of cognitive dissonance is when feminists fail to criticise Islamic states like Saudi Arabia for oppressing women even though they are committed to equal rights for both sexes. The fact that Islamic fundamentalism disadvantages women is ignored on the basis we must celebrate diversity and difference (the new code for multiculturalism) because all cultures are equal.

57. **Collective privilege.** Barry McWang on Twitter describes this as follows: "According to today's geniuses, if your share

a gender, skin colour, or cultural heritage with anyone who was – at any point – privileged, then so are you. Even if you're dirt poor". An example of collective privilege involves disadvantaged working-class British children being criticised as privileged because they are white.

58. **Colourism.** *The Oxford Dictionary* defines colourism as "Prejudice or discrimination against individuals with a dark skin tone, typically among people of the same ethnic or racial group". Examples include dark skinned Indian women using cosmetics to lighten their skin and Chinese women using skin care products designed to make them look more like pale skinned Westerners. On the Independent website Georgina Lawton uses as an example of colourism black men preferring to marry light skinned black women. Rather than condemning such men she argues it is not their fault as it's "undoubtably a symptom of racism, which was in no way created within minority communities by men. Indeed, the most pernicious side effects of light-skin privilege are seen to be upheld by the global white supremacist capitalist patriarchy and that negatively affects both male and female people of colour".

59. **Competition.** Competing against others and being ranked in terms of performance breeds inequality, reinforces disadvantage and favours the wealthy. The Australian Education Union argues "Reliance on competition is a primary cause of

inequalities of educational outcome because students from certain social groups are advantaged by competitive selection methods. Competitive selection also sets students against each other rather than encouraging co-operative learning methods" (AEU '1998 Curriculum Policy').

Andrew Hamilton on *The Eureka* website condemns competition as it "makes strangers out of friends (and causes) fear and envy to dominate love, the desire to possess, to master the desire to give, and individual desires to trump common needs, and reduces public conversation to conflict between interest groups with the rewards going to the most powerful. In a word, a world enslaved by competition is uncivilized".

60. **Compulsory heterosexuality.** Defined by the encyclopedia of glbtq culture as "the assumption that women and men are innately attracted to each other emotionally and sexually and that heterosexuality is normal and universal... in our society this leads to an institutionalized inequality of power". After referring to the writings of Adrienne Rich the dictionary states that this binary concept "is an institution designed to perpetuate male social and economic privilege".

61. **Confirmation bias.** Refers to the tendency to agree with and approve of ideas, arguments and information that confirm already established ideas and beliefs. Confirmation bias is a characteristic of Eurocentric, white, privileged males and it never occurs with those who are woke and politically correct.

62. **Constructivism.** The Australian Commonwealth's report 'Teaching Reading' defines constructivism as "a theory of learning that builds on the work of Piaget, Bruner and Vygotsky, which views students as inherently active, self-regulating learners who construct knowledge cooperatively with other learners in developmentally appropriate ways... Adoption of a constructivist approach in the classroom involves a shift from predominantly teacher-directed methods to student-centred, active discovery learning and immersion approaches via cooperative group work, discussion focused on investigations and problem solving".

Constructivism can also be traced back to the American educator John Dewey and the French philosopher Jean-Jacques Rousseau – both who argue learning should be natural, centred on the world of the child and where the teacher is seen as a "facilitator" and "guide by the side". The New South Wales academic John Sweller argues that even though this progressive approach to learning has dominated Australian and American education since the late '60s it is ineffective and responsible for falling standards. Sweller argues in favour of explicit teaching where students are expected to master what is essential until it can be re-called automatically and teachers have greater authority and control.

63. **Cooking with gas.** An obsolete expression before people were woke as they still believed gas provided an cost effective, reliable and beneficial method of cooking and home heating.

64. **Conversion ideology.** Defined by gender activists as the belief imposed by heteronormative, transphobic people and institutions, especially religious, that transgenderism is unnatural, harmful and immoral. According to trans-activists conversion ideology is used to justify damaging and life-threatening conversion practices like parents and priests counselling against transitioning.

65. **Conversion therapy.** Involves counselling, advising or warning against trying to change one's biological sex. Transgender activists argue conversion therapy is always harmful and unjustified as gender and sexuality are fluid and limitless. Everyone, even children and adolescents, have the right to choose whether they are LGBTIQ+ or anything in between. Increasingly, governments are legislating to ban conversion theory even if it involves practices like counseling and prayer.

66. **Coon cheese.** Coon Cheese has been popular with Australians for countless years but in 2020, after pressure from Indigenous activists, it was rebranded as Cheer Cheese. Even though the cheese was named after its inventor, Edward William Coon, it was attacked as racist. Other examples of product names reinforcing unconscious bias and structural sexism and racism include White Knights, Redskins, Chicos and Colonial Beer.

67. **Corporatocracy.** Parnell Palme McGuiness (*The Age*, 24 April 2021) describes this as the dangers inherent in businesses

and corporations seeking to influence political decisions. She writes, as a result of businesses arguing against legislation in the United States directed at making voting more transparent: "Regardless of the merits of the legislation... if the *Times* ad were to affect policy making, we might ask why the US should trouble with elections at all. Why not simply give large companies power to take decisions on behalf of the whole country?" After noting that corporations generally act unilaterally without seeking the views of employees, McGuinness writes "in the age of corporate activism, does democracy as we celebrate it still have a chance?"

68. **Cow's milk.** The activist group People for the Ethical Treatment of Animals (PETA) argues cow's milk should not be consumed as "dairy milk has long been a symbol of white supremacy". The group's website argues "Rape is perhaps the single most heinous crime involving both power and violence. But it's standard procedure in the dairy industry. Like all mammals, cows produce milk only during and after pregnancy, so roughly every nine months, cows on dairy farms are forcibly impregnated so that their milk production will continue. They're restrained on what the farmers themselves call 'rape racks' while insemination instruments are shoved into their vaginas".

69. **Critical race theory.** Helen Pluckrose and James Lindsay in their book *Cynical Theories* define critical race theory

as the belief "race is a social construct that was created to maintain white privilege and white supremacy". CRT is based on the assumption there is nothing redeeming or positive about Western civilisation as societies like America, the UK and Australia are riven with structural racism, white supremacism and have a history of imperialism and colonial exploitation.

70. **Critical theory.** Originating in the Frankfurt School in Germany during the 1920s critical theory involves evaluating and critiquing capitalism to unmask how those in control oppress and marginalise the disadvantaged and the dispossessed. The Marxist academics involved realised the communist revolution was never going to occur in the West through violence and that the focus had to shift from economic issues to the battle of ideas and the long march through the institutions like universities and schools, the church, family and the media. As argued by Australian academic Wanda Skowronska in a paper titled '1960s psychologists: beguiling ideologues and smiling assassins': "Critical theory did not aim to tear down the economic base of western society as, with the force of history, it was inevitably going to collapse anyway. It aimed rather at tearing down the cultural superstructure which supposedly reflected the powerful controllers of the economic system and this would enable the collapse of western civilisation".

Critical theory now involves a rainbow alliance of

theories including: neo-Marxism, postmodernism, deconstructionism and feminist, gender, queer and post-colonial theories. Even though Western civilisation is responsible for record levels of prosperity, health, stability and freedom as well as miraculous advances in medicine, science and technology it is considered inherently sexist, heteronormative, exploitive, Eurocentric and guilty of reinforcing inequality and disadvantage.

71. **Critical literacy.** On offshoot of critical theory, critical literacy is an approach to English teaching based on the work of the South American Marxist educator Paulo Freire. His books *Pedagogy of the Oppressed* and *Education: The Practice of Freedom* have had a profound effect on how reading is taught and how literature is analysed and evaluated. Central to Freire's work is the belief that education should be empowering and liberating and directed at challenging the status quo and changing society.

Freire argues the true purpose of education is to allow students "to perceive themselves in dialectical relationship with their social reality (and) to assume an increasingly critical attitude toward the world and so to transform it". Practices like rote learning, teachers as experts and failing to address real-life issues are criticised as promoting a "banking concept" where learners, supposedly, are passive and treated as empty vessels waiting to be filled with knowledge. The Australian Association for the Teaching of English and the Australian Curriculum Studies Association are strong advocates of critical literacy and argue that English as a subject must be a vehicle to deconstruct texts in terms of power relationships and to empower so-called victim groups: including women, LGBTIQ+ people, people of colour, migrants and the working class.

72. **Crumb maiden.** The *Urban Dictionary* describes crumb maidens "as a person (Male or Female) who works to maintain power structures (Typically gendered power structures) which hurt them and/or their community in the hope that they can gather some small residual benefit".

73. **Culinary white supremacy.** Involves white people serving food traditionally associated with people of colour. Examples include white people cooking tacos, Peking duck and Tandoori chicken.

74. **Cultural appropriation.** The Australian *HuffPost* defines this as "the act of taking or using things from a culture that is not your own, especially without showing that you understand or respect this culture". Examples include a Perth mother making the mistake of allowing her white, privileged son to dress as his hero, the AFL footballer of colour Nic Naitanui, for a school dress up day. For this the mother was condemned and her son expelled from the party for disrespecting the "Other". Hollywood is especially

susceptible to claims of cultural appropriation witnessed by Scarlet Johansson forced to withdraw from playing the role of a transgender character. On Twitter Elise Bauman criticised Johansson arguing "the way you can use your privilege as a white Ciswoman is to amplify the voices of underrepresented communities, not speak for them". The famous Shakespearean actor Sir Lawrence Olivier is guilty of cultural appropriation as one of his most famous roles is playing the person of colour Othello. Another example of cultural appropriation is Peter Sellers playing the role of an accident prone Indian in the Hollywood movie *The Party*. (Note: criticisms related to cultural appropriation do not apply to the woke – evidenced by a black American actor playing the Scottish nobleman in Shakespeare's *Macbeth*.)

75. **Cultural curtain.** The indigenous academic Anthony Dillion explains this as white academics, politicians and blacktivists always blaming Indigenous disadvantage on cultural factors. Western societies like Australia are structurally racist and guilty of oppressing Aboriginal and Torres Strait Island people who once lived a utopian existence before the arrival of Europeans. Instead of endorsing identity politics and victimhood Dillion argues Indigenous people have personal agency and need to be treated the same as white Australians. Instead of focusing on division and treating Indigenous Australians as a separate race Dillion argues we should "celebrate oneness and connectedness".

76. **Cultural genocide.** Anthony Dillion details how the expression is used by blacktivists when arguing anyone who disagrees the First Fleet was an invasion and that Australia is inherently racist is guilty of promoting cultural genocide.

77. **Cultural Marxism.** Whereas classical Marxism focuses on overthrowing capitalism by taking control of the modes and means of production cultural Marxism emphasises transforming society by engaging in the culture wars. (See also critical theory and the Frankfurt School.)

78. **Culture Wars.** The expression is used to describe the ongoing cultural battle between neo-Marxist inspired cultural-left ideologues and activists and those conservatives committed to defending Western civilisation, the ongoing debt owed to Judeo-Christianity and concepts like rationality, impartiality and reason. (See also critical theory, Cultural Marxism and the Frankfurt School.)

79. **Dead naming.** This involves referring to the previous gender of a person who has undergone transition from male to female or female to male. The American Wikileaks whistle blower Chelsea Manning, the American soldier convicted of treason for leaking secret documents, after undergoing transition to a woman, refuses to be addressed according to her previous gender. As reported by the ABC on being interviewed by Peter Greste who referred to Manning's pre-

transition gender names/pronouns Manning interrupted Greste saying "please don't deadname me".

80. **Deaf as a post.** Considered offensive to the hearing impaired as it suggests they have the same hearing qualities as a wooden post.

81. **Decolonise language.** Dr Kirstin Small, a Queensland specialist medical lecturer at Griffith University, argues medical names like "Achilles heel" and "Adam's apple" privilege men and are no longer acceptable. Dr Kisha Khnot, a council member The Royal Australian and New Zealand College of Obstetricians and Gynaecologists, agrees arguing "In medicine many body parts are named from people from many centuries ago, even ancient kings and heroes and gods. Women don't get a look in". Dr Khnot gives the example of hysterectomy which is associated with female hysteria being changed to uterectomy (Queensland's *Sunday Mail*, 18 July 2020).

82. **Decolonising the curriculum.** James Lindsay in his essay 'Decolonizing the curriculum' describes the rationale for this radical process as: "the prevailing mindset of the activists is that the curriculum was colonized by the presumption that white, Western epistemologies and pedagogies are unjustly favored over 'other' ways of knowing and teaching".

83. **Deconstruction.** Often attributed to the French academic Jacques Derrida deconstruction, in the words of *The Cambridge Dictionary*, involves analysing "a text in order to show there is no fixed meaning but that it can be understood in a different way by each reader". The meaning of a text varies from person to person as the encounter is subjective; there is no authorial intention as the author is non-existent (as in dead) and words have no inherent meaning as they are simply "signifiers" that mean different things to different people.

84. **Deep fake.** A malicious hoax perpetrated on the internet using digitally altered pictures, videos and sound falsely proving somebody is guilty of a crime or offence never committed. Also used to sexualise celebrity movie stars and to portray politicians saying things they would never say.

85. **Defenestrated.** *The Cambridge Dictionary* defines defenestrated as "the action of throwing or pushing someone out of a window", the word also can mean "the action of forcing someone, especially a leader, out of his or her job". One example is the British FA Chairman Greg Clarke being forced to resign after using the expression "coloured footballers" when being questioned by members of parliament. Clarke was also guilty of suggesting being gay was a "lifestyle choice".

86. **Degenderize.** Refers to expunging heteronormative gender specific pronouns and descriptions. The City of Berkeley in

California revised its municipal code in 2019 to "replace all instances of gendered pronouns with the singular 'they'... and to indicate that whenever a gender-neutral pronoun is used, it shall be deemed to include the feminine and the masculine also". The city officials argue "broadening social awareness of transgender and gender nonconforming identities has brought to light the importance of non-binary gender inclusivity".

87. **Demisexual.** A sexual attraction only experienced when people are emotionally close.

88. **Denier.** A description used by cultural-left activists to condemn and silence anyone who questions or contradicts politically correct orthodoxy in relation to issues such as: man-made global warming, multiculturalism, gender and sexuality and feminism. As in "everyone knows the science is proven when it comes to man-made global warming and those who disagree like the scientists associated with the UK based Global Warming Policy Foundation are wrong; they are climate deniers".

89. **Detransitioners.** Refers to those born male or female who transitioned later in life but who now want to reverse the procedure. While radical gender activists forcefully promote the benefits of transgenderism there is little, if any, acknowledgement that detransitioners exist. The Society

for Evidence Based Gender Medicine suggests it is a "poorly understood phenomenon". In a survey of 237 participants the reasons for detransitioning "was most often tied to the realization that their gender dysphoria was related to other issues (70%), health concerns (62%), and the fact that transition did not alleviate their dysphoria (50%)". The gender fluidity Safe School program makes no mention of the reality that many who undertake chemical and/or surgical transitioning later change their minds.

90. **Digital natives.** School children are no longer described as students with the expectation they be taught by teachers (otherwise known as "guides by the side" or "facilitators"). As a result of the digital revolution the printed word is obsolete as millennials have been surrounded by computers, mobile phones, laptops, social networking sites and screens since birth. Old fashioned learning and knowledge is outdated as students are now "knowledge navigators" where searching the web offers unlimited information and possibilities for exploration. Digital natives through a process of collaborative, negotiated goal setting and inquiry-based, self-directed learning are free to explore the world-wide web making teachers redundant.

Ignored is the research carried out by the Organisation for Economic Co-operation and Development concluding an over reliance on the new technologies is counter-productive as standards suffer and students under-perform as measured by international tests such as PISA. Developments in cognitive psychology also suggest an over reliance on screens, especially during childhood, scrambles the brain and impairs learning.

91. **Disability shaming.** Abusing or making fun of those who are disabled. (See also ableism.)

92. **Dissing.** Originally associated with the American hip hop scene dissing involves showing disrespect and insulting someone. As in "you are so fat you must have shares in McDonalds".

93. **Disprivileged.** Involves getting students to carry out a survey to identify who are privileged and who are oppressed and disadvantaged by mainstream capitalist, white, Eurocentric and misogynist society. Juliet Moses in the Australian edition of *The Spectator* details a privilege worksheet given to students at an American high school in which they add or sub-track points according to their religion, ethnicity, skin colour, sexuality and gender. Those who are white, Christian, male and able-bodied score highest as they are privileged. If you are black, gay, Muslim, a woman or genderqueer you score minus points thus proving you are disprivileged as Western, capitalist and Eurocentric societies like America oppress and marginalise those who are not mainstream.

94. **Diversity gaffe.** Refers to the unwoke making a statement or comment, often unknowingly, that is politically incorrect and offensive. Examples include using the wrong description when talking about non-white people, suggesting that marriage involves a man and a woman and using expressions like "dumb as a doorpost" and "blind as a bat".

95. **Diversity Toolkits.** An example of a diversity toolkit is the Flinders University's 'Cultural Diversity and Inclusive Practice (CDIP) Toolkit'. The purpose of the toolkit is "to sustain and enhance a culturally inclusive environment at Flinders University. Cultural diversity refers to the similarities and differences among cultures across ethnic, religious and language boundaries, for example". Whereas universities once prioritised the search for knowledge, wisdom and truth based on Western concepts of reason and rationality the focus is now on diversity and difference, identity politics and victimhood. The Toolkit defines students in terms of their "national, racial, ethnic, religious and language origins" instead of what they hold in common as university students pursuing tertiary studies.

96. **Dog whistling.** On the website of the American-based VOX media organ-isation, Ian Olasov describes dog whistling as "political shorthand for a phrase that may sound innocuous to some people, but which also communicates something more insidious either to a subset of the audience or outside

of the audience's conscious awareness – a covert appeal to some noxious set of views". Olasov list three types of dog whistling: semantic, contextual, and stereotype-dependent as well as arguing centre-right politicians like President Trump often use dog whistling to gains voter support.

97. **Doomscrolling (also known as doomsurfing).** Refers to those addicted to surfing the net and checking the media even though the news, events and issues are depressing, unsettling and guaranteed to promote negativity and bad karma.

98. **Doxed.** Refers to a victim of doxing – as in "someone found an old picture of me at a dress up party wearing a tribal costume – I've been doxed".

99. **Doxing.** Involves gathering personal information and data about individuals, usually from social networking sites, and making it public on the internet without their knowledge or permission. Doxing is often used to shame, vilify and attack individuals and groups and has the power to go viral in a short time and is difficult, if not impossible, to counter.

100. **Dunny man.** A now obsolete term once used to describe men whose job was to dispose of human excrement before the installation of proper sewerage disposal. Now seen as offensive as demeaning and phallocentric; the preferred alternative is "a non-gendered, sanitation person" or "non-binary hygiene worker".

101. **DWEMs.** The 1992 American publication titled The *Official Politically Correct Dictionary & Handbook* defines DWEMs as "dead, white, European males" responsible for the evils and sins committed by Western civilisation. As argued by the 150 Sydney University academics opposed to establishing a Western Civilisation Centre funded by the Ramsay bequest, teaching about Western civilisation promotes "European supremacism" and a "conservative, culturally essentialist and Eurocentric vision".

102. **Earth mother.** Environmental activists who worship the Gaia describe the planet as the earth mother based on the belief nature is benevolent and nurturing. Worshiping the earth mother can be traced back to ancient pre-Christian pagan rituals and more recently the 1960s counter-culture Aquarius youth movement. Gavin Ashenden in the *Catholic Weekly* describes the deep-green environmental movement as motivated by "a new religious instinct".

103. **Easter worshippers.** After Christian churches in Sri Lanka were bombed and hundreds of Christians killed while celebrating the death and ascension of Jesus, President Obama and Hilary Clinton instead of acknowledging Christianity described the attack as one involving "Easter worshippers". Critics suggest this is yet another PC example of christianophobia.

104. **Ecofascism/ecofascist.** The *Urban Dictionary* defines ecofascism as someone "who advocates for the subordination of individual self-interest to the ecofundamentalism of the Green lobby". In its most extreme form ecofascism relies on threats, intimidation and violence to achieve its ultimate goal of ridding personkind's destructive impact on nature. An example of ecofascism is the Aussie Farms website making public the locations of homes and farms of primary producers across Australia and inciting protestors to invade properties involved in animal husbandry.

105. **Eco-anxiety.** The Macquarie Dictionary describes this as "Feelings of distress and fear brought on by the effects of climate change". It's not usual for young girls to decry the fact, because of man-made global warming, they will never have children as the world is about to end because of man-made climate change.

106. **Ecocide.** The Duke and Duchess of Sussex, otherwise known as Harry and Meghan, use the word "ecocide" to refer to what they see at a series of overlapping ecological disasters now occurring across the globe. Examples include bushfires in Australia and California as well as the destruction of the Amazon forests plus carbon induced global warming causing droughts. All symptoms of global warming caused largely by fossil fuels.

107. **Emotional labour.** Gemma Hartley in a piece published in *Harper's Bazaar* uses the expression to describe the added burden women face at home. Hartley argues as well as physical labour such women are responsible for emotional labour; she writes "It's so exhausting and frustrating to be the manager of the household and the manager of everyone's emotional state". As noted by Mary Ward in *The Age*, the term is now used "as a catch-all for gendered labour inequality, particularly in domestic partnerships".

108. **Environmental racism.** An Indian climate activist living in Bangalore, who follows Greta Thunberg, argues "People of colour are suffering from the climate crisis first-hand – a lot of people don't give us attention that we need. The fact that you would choose to listen to a white person on the same issue rather than a person of colour, to me, is environmental racism".

109. **Equality of outcomes.** In opposition to equality of opportunity (where all are given the same opportunity to succeed based on merit and ability) equality of outcomes involves positive discrimination and affirmative action for victim groups. Imposing quotas to mandate the percentage of women in parliament or the percentage of women on company boards is a policy based on achieving equality of outcomes. In the United States there is positive discrimination for people of colour for entry to colleges and universities (except Asian

students who are penalised for achieving academic success based on their ability and efforts).

110. **Erisology.** The Swedish blogger John Nerst uses the term, taken from the Greek goddess of discord Eris, to describe the way disagreement and debate is now characterised by violent argument, discord and vitriol.

111. **Esky.** In Australia "Esky" is a brand name for a famous portable cooler that has been condemned as an example of cultural appropriation. Tom Cowie in *The Age* (12/1/2020) writes Esky is short for Eskimo – "It's a term for people who live in and around the Arctic that is now considered by many to be offensive, though it is still used in places like Alaska".

112. **Eskimo Pie.** A much-loved ice cream that is guilty of cultural appropriation and unconscious racism. In Australia Eskimo Pie has been renamed Polar Pie. Ignored is that appropriating the names Polar is seen by woke activists as offensive to Polar Bears.

113. **Eurocentric.** As a result of post-colonial theory it is no longer acceptable to acknowledge or celebrate the achievements of those countries associated with Europe and the United Kingdom. Instead of celebrating the grand narrative associated with Western civilisation, a narrative that can be traced back to ancient Egypt, Rome and Greece, the West's legacy is oppressive and responsible for colonial

exploitation and imperialism as well as climate change, the destruction of the world's ecosystem and the death of countless non-human species.

114. **Eye candy.** A sexist and demeaning expression used by misogynist men to describe women seen to be alluring and sexually attractive.

115. **Facilitators.** In the 21st century classroom teachers are described as facilitators as their expertise as teachers is no longer needed. Students, otherwise known as "knowledge navigators" and "digital natives", are involved in self-directed, inquiry-based learning in an ever transient, digital, 21st century, global environment.

116. **Faith-phobia.** An extreme hatred and dislike of religious beliefs, especially Christianity, and the conviction there is no place for religion in public debates and government policy and decision-making. Even though parliaments across Australia begin with the Lord's prayer and the Australian Constitution refers to "Almighty God" cultural-left critics argue Australia is a secular society and religious freedoms, in particular, must be curtailed. Except for events like Christmas and Easter when secular critics enjoy their holidays and are happy to take advantage of family reunions, celebrations and time off work.

117. **False consciousness.** The Italian Marxist Antonio Gramsci argues that capitalist society is able to reproduce itself and maintain dominance and control by making unequal power relations appear acceptable and normal. As a result of false consciousness girls and boys might appear happy being Cisfemales and Cismales but this is only because society indoctrinates them with the belief that heterosexuality is preferable to being LGBTIQ+.

Girls who look forward to marriage, bearing children and being mothers and wives only do so because they live in a patriarchal society where what is expected and acceptable is determined by men to suit their selfish ends. Workers who are well paid, who achieve a high standard of living and lead a prosperous life, if only they were intelligent enough to realise, are being oppressed because of false consciousness. The reality is that they are disadvantaged and are being exploited by an inherently unjust and inequitable capitalist system.

118. **Fast fashion.** Refers to those clothing companies and fashion houses employing unethical practices and cheap labour.

119. **Fat shaming.** In *You Have the Right to Remain Fat: A Manifesto*, Virgie Tovar argues fat people are unfairly ostracised and made fun of because of fatness – otherwise known as being horizontally challenged. Tovar defines fatphobia as fat-shaming those who fail to conform to the "ideal" body image imposed by a binary, heteronormative,

capitalist, consumer driven society. The Commonwealth Minister for Sport, Bridget McKenzie, recently was accused of fat shaming when she mimicked having a bloated stomach while launching an Obesity campaign. She later apologised saying "I sincerely apologise for this very unfortunate photo taken as I demonstrated how my stomach felt after scrambled eggs reacted (with) yoghurt I had just eaten".

120. **Father Christmas.** A mythical figure created to dupe unsuspecting children with the belief if they are subservient and comply with the authoritarian demands of their parents they will be rewarded. (See also Santa Claus.)

121. **Father's Day.** A phallocentric, binary ritual that privileges heterosexuality and the mistaken belief that children need to have a biological father. Alternative descriptions include "A Non-binary, Gender Free Person's Day" and "Parents and Carers Day".

122. **Female.** An oppressive binary description of women that reinforces male dominance and the patriarchal nature of capitalist, phallocentric society. The description also offends those self-identifying as non-gender, gender diverse, queer or in transition. A Monash University diversity guide warns against using the expression "female" as it is a "term that can be applied to animals and objects".

123. **Female colonisation.** Vania Phitidis on the HuffPost website argues as a result of false consciousness women fail to realise how they perceive themselves and self-identify is controlled by "patriarchy and capitalism". Women no longer control their bodies as they have been colonised by men only concerned with profit making and dominating women by enforcing a sexist, oppressive stereotype.

124. **Female assigned at birth.** Used to describe an individual's birth-sex on the basis, instead of being biologically determined, that traditional binary sex categories are restrictive social constructs imposed on innocent and unsuspecting babies by a heteronormative, transphobic society (also known as female bodied).

125. **Feminism.** While there are various version of feminism (generally categorised as first, second and third wave) what all have in common is the belief that society is patriarchal and phallocentric where men dominate and women are oppressed and victimised. More extreme feminists argue men are inherently misogynist and violent towards women.

126. **Feminist Porn.** Janet Albrechtsen (*The Australian*, 25–26 September 2021) describes this as a genre of television series focusing on "fascinating female characters, full of nuance, complication and unpredictable character turns and men who are as interesting as a lump of cement".

127. **Femme.** The Californian Scripps College diversity and inclusion Glossary of Terms describes Femme as "gender identity in which someone (female, male or other) has an awareness of cultural standards of femininity and actively embodies a feminine appearance, role, or archetype. It is usually – but not always – associated with a gay or queer sexual identity/sexuality".

128. **Fillies.** A term used to describe female horses but politically incorrect when applied to women as sometimes happens in racing circles. Melissa Singer argues describing young ladies at the racetrack as fillies "reduces their participation in the sport to that of playthings and walking coat hangers and does little to advance gender equality". Singer also suggests that using descriptions like "sheilas, chicks, birds, girls, woozas, bitches" is also unacceptable as such labels "are often degrading, demeaning and, in worst cases, downright abusive".

129. **First Fleet.** Refers to the 11 ships and over 1480 men, women and children under the control of Admiral Arthur Phillip that arrived in what is now Sydney in 1788 to establish a British penal colony. While the event is officially celebrated on the 26th of January as the birth of modern-day Australia, critics describe it as an invasion leading to genocide. (See also Australia Day.)

130. **First nations.** While nations is a Eurocentric concept employed to subjugate others and is foreign to the over 600 to 700 different Indigenous tribes that existed when the First Fleet arrived in Botany Bay it has been appropriated by Aboriginal activists in their battle for constitutional recognition. As the expression 'First nations' originated in Canada to describe its first inhabitants by employing the term Aboriginal activists are open to the charge of cultural appropriation.

131. **Flamed.** Refers to being personally attacked, vilified and abused in an online forum or via the internet and other digital media.

132. **Flight shaming.** Environmental activists argue that people should either restrict or stop flying as aeroplanes are significant contributors to global warming. The Swedish activist Bjorn Ferry suggests that those who fly unnecessarily are immoral and, as a result, in Europe those who fly regularly are publicly shamed. An exception to flight shaming are the hundreds of environmental government officials, scientists and activists flying around the world on a regular basis to attend global warming events and conferences. Those wealthy businessmen, celebrities, politicians and bureaucrats attending exclusive talkfests like the Davos World Economic Forum are also excluded from being flight shamed.

133. **Frankfurt School.** The Marxist inspired academics who established the Frankfurt School in Germany during the 1920s are responsible for developing critical theory – an approach to sociology, economics, history and philosophy that has led to a radical alliance of cultural-left theories, including: Neo-Marxism, extreme feminism, postmodernism, deconstructionism and gender, queer and post-colonial theories. (See also critical theory.) Michael Gove, the former UK Secretary of State for Education, argues in his book *Celsius 7/7* the thinkers of the Frankfurt School revised Marxism as primarily a cultural rather than an economic movement. In place of anger at traditional capitalism, scorn was directed at the reigning values of the West.

134. **Fun police.** The American commentator Bill Maher criticises politically correct fun police for decreeing there be "no hula girls, no Indian chiefs, no Southern belles, no ninjas, gypsies" during Halloween. Maher goes on to argue "Not everything that merely alludes to another culture is racist, or cultural appropriation" and that "Halloween was always fun because it wasn't PC. Not being PC was almost the whole point of the holiday. But now everything has to turn into a federal case of snowflakes v. humor".

135. **Gammon.** A British term used to insult conservative, centre-right politicians and spokesmen whose anger and prejudice gives their faces a red colouring (the colour of gammon).

136. **Gaslighting.** Trans-activists describe gaslighting as heteronormative parents causing trans-children to doubt their desire to transgender. For example, instead of parents questioning a child's decision to adopt a non-binary, fluid gender identity they should be positive and celebrate the fact. The *Urban Dictionary* describes gaslighting as "A form of psychological abuse, sometimes called ambient abuse, where false information is presented to a victim, making them doubt their own memory, perception and quite often their sanity".

137. **Gay.** The Monash University Diversity and Inclusion Guide defines Gay as "a person often a man, who forms their primary loving and sexual relationships with others of the same gender". Gay is often used as a heteronormative insult by Cisgender people and, as a result, the line "gay your life must be" in the song *Kookaburra Sits on the Old Gum Tree* has been changed to "Fun your life must be".

138. **Gaydar.** The 'OMG I'm Queer' booklet produced for the Safe Schools program defines "gaydar" as the ability to tell if someone is gay. Students are warned, though, that "Unless you see someone sucking face with their same sex partner, or they tell you their sexuality, your gaydar isn't going to be exactly accurate".

139. **Gender.** The 'Gender Questioning' booklet defines gender as follows "Gender can refer to biological sex, social roles or gender identity. There are many genders, however

the most commonly recognised are male or female". The authors go on to argue "There are no limitations on what your gender and identity can be". The academic behind the Safe Schools gender and sexuality program, Roz Ward, argues that gender is a social construct imposed by capitalism. Ward goes on the argue "Marxism offers both the hope and the strategy needed to create a world where human sexuality, gender and how we relate to our bodies can blossom in extraordinary new and amazing ways that we can only try to imagine today".

Any attempt to define gender in terms of a person's biological sex at birth is considered oppressive and guilty of enforcing heteronormativity. After the Trump administration in America signalled that gender would be determined by one's genitalia at birth Sarah Warbelow, the legal director of the Human Rights Campaign which campaigns for the rights of lesbian, gay, bisexual and transgender people, argued "Transgender people are frightened... At every step where the administration has had the choice, they've opted to turn their back on transgender people."

The South Australian school curriculum some years ago, under the heading of "Gender Equity" argues "Running through all the issues brought to light in investigating gender as a societal construct is the categorisation of the norm and the other with the other not being up to standard. Examples include the male/female, reason/emotion, sciences/humanities, public/private and paid/unpaid work splits. This persistent ordering into dichotomies shores up the norm in the dominant power relation to the other and is often not explicitly examined in curriculum, teaching and learning. Curriculum can continue to express these power relations or take part in their deconstruction and reconstruction".

140. **Gender coding.** The Encyclopedia of Adolescence defines gender coding as "the signals that individuals manifest externally and that indicate their sexuality or relative masculinity or femininity. Individuals may use their outward appearance to communicate implicitly gender identity and Sex Roles and Gender Roles, or use their appearance to avoid doing so. Gender coding can reflect a wide spectrum of sex differences". As a result of radical gender theory, instead of being binary and heteronormative, gender coding can be fluid, dynamic and limitless.

141. **Gender deafness.** One-time Australian Foreign Affairs Minister Julie Bishop describes gender deafness as the way men during meetings, after ignoring a woman's contribution, accept what was said when the same point is made by a man. The Sky News commentator and one-time chief of staff to Prime Minister Tony Abbott during the time Bishop was a minister argues this never occurred in the cabinet room and describes Bishop's complaints as "victim revisionism".

142. **Gender fairy story book.** The author Jo Hirst describes this picture book as "designed for young children aged four years and up" that tells of a non-binary gender fairy who explains to children that "there are more identities than just male or female". Those committed to gender theory argue that traditional fairy tales like *Cinderella* and *Snow White* are guilty of heteronormativity as the happy ending privileges the love between a woman and a man.

The American actress, Kristen Bell, after reading *Snow White* to her daughters is reported as asking them "Don't you think that it's weird that the prince kisses Snow White without her permission? Because you cannot kiss someone if they're sleeping!". The British actress Keira Knightley is also concerned about the dangerous impact of traditional fairy tales and argues *Cinderella*, for example, portrays a girl unable to act decisively as she relies on the prince to rescue her.

143. **Gender identity.** The Sex Discrimination Amendment Act 2013 defines gender identity as "the gender-related identity, appearance or mannerisms or other gender-related characteristics of a person (whether by way of medical intervention or not) with or without regard to the person's designated sex at birth". Material associated with the Safe Schools program argues that while you might be born with the physical characteristics of one of two sexes (girl or boy) there is no reason to believe this defines your gender. Gender

is fluid and non-binary and how you express your gender is "a personal thing, everyone does it, and everyone does it differently". The Tasmanian parliament's lower house recently passed legislation allowing gender neutral birth certificates as well as legislating to allow teenagers over 16 to self-identify their gender simply by signing a statutory declaration.

144. **Gender incongruence.** Whereas the expression gender dysphoria implies some kind of mental and/or emotional disorder the description gender incongruence is less discriminatory and judgemental as it relates to a person's decision to transition away from the sexual identity they were assigned at birth.

145. **Gender mainstreaming.** The United Nations Entity for Gender Equality and the Empowerment of Women describes this as "ensuring that gender perspectives and attention to the goal of gender equality are central to all activities – policy development, research, advocacy/ dialogue, legislation, resource allocation, and planning, implementation and monitoring of programmes and projects".

146. **Gender neutral toilets.** Refers to any toilet, sometimes described as "unisex", that does not specify male or female use. The Safe Schools booklet 'OMG I'M Trans' states that "Victoria has no explicit laws about using public bathrooms and you can use whichever ones you want". The Safe

Schools booklet also argues that schools should provide gender neutral toilets for boys and girls who self-identify other than their birth sex or who are in transition.

147. **Gender normative.** The belief that because the overwhelming majority of people self-identify as female or male that heterosexuality is the norm. *The Meriam Webster Dictionary* defines gender normative as "adhering to or reinforcing ideal standards of masculinity or femininity". The 98% of Australians who self-identify as female or male are guilty of being gender normative.

148. **Gender policing.** Refers to enforcing normative gender expressions in relation to a person who is perceived as not participating in behaviour that aligns with their assigned gender at birth.

149. **Gender pronouns/Inclusive language.** The Monash University guide to inclusive language recommends replacing gender specific pronouns like "he" or "she" with gender neutral alternatives like "they" or "zie". Asking students their Christian name is also politically incorrect as the Monash guide argues "Terms like 'Christian name' should be replaced by 'first name' for the obvious reason that the person in question may not be Christian". The University of Melbourne's language guide goes one step further arguing that using the terms "first name" and

"Christian name" reflects "a bias towards Christian, Anglo-Celtic culture". A Qantas staff guide recommends against using heteronormative descriptions like "husband" and "wife", preferring instead "spouse" or "partner".

150. **Gendered AI voices.** Ellie Zolfagharifard in *The Age* (August 2020) argues AI voices used by smart speakers including Siri and Amazon's Alexa reinforce gender stereotyping as they involve a woman's voice. She quotes UN research that argues using female voices suggests woman are "obliging, docile and eager to please helpers, available at the touch of a button".

151. **Genderless fashion.** As the expression suggests genderless fashion involves designing clothes and accessories that no longer adopt a binary, heteronormative and oppressive view of fashion where there are distinctive styles suited to women, men and those identifying as non-binary and/or genderless.

152. **Genderqueer.** The *GLBTQ Encyclopedia* defines genderqueer individuals as those "who feel that their gender identities and/or gender expressions do not correspond to the gender assigned to them at birth, but who do not want to transition to the 'opposite' gender. Characterizing themselves as neither female nor male, as both, or as somewhere in between, genderqueers challenge binary constructions of gender and traditional images of transgender people". Other

descriptions include gender diverse, transboi, boydyke, third gendered, bi-gendered, multi-gendered, androgyne, and gender bender.

153. **Gender reveal parties.** Instead of discovering a baby's sex at birth many parents hold gender reveal parties beforehand to announce the expected child's sex. Such parties have been condemned as reinforcing gender stereotyping and reinforcing a binary, heteronormative view of sex and gender.

154. **Girl boss.** Marnie Vinall (*The Age*, 2 March 2021) defines "girl boss" as "a confident, capable woman who pursues her own ambitions instead of working for others or otherwise settling in life". Vinall criticises this view of feminism as focusing on "individual success and power" instead of exposing the "structural and systematic inequality" experienced by non-white, marginalised women. After referring to the American author Koa Beck, Vinall writes this inherently middle-class, privileged view of feminism is "often presented through a white, heterosexual, able-bodied lens – frames the individual rather than the collective as the agent of change".

155. **Global stilling.** Describes the phenomena recently observed involving a reduction in surface wind speed. The concern is any reduction in wind speeds will adversely affect the increasing reliance on wind driven power generation.

156. **Gonzo pornography.** *Urban Dictionary* describes this as a "type of pornography that attempts to place the viewer directly into the scene via a POV camera angle". The effect emphasises subjectivity and heightens the viewer's excitement and arousal.

157. **Goosed.** According to *Urban Dictionary* 'goosed' refers to being sexually molested or assaulted and the expression is common in the British acting industry. Dame Judi Dench, an unreconstructed Cisfemale, states when she first started acting being goosed behind the scenes was common and that "There was a time at the Old Vic when if you weren't goosed as you went in there was something wrong with you".

158. **Greenwash.** A term used to describe companies and corporations that disguise their environmental destructive character by presenting themselves as ecologically sound and green. As in the mining giant BHP marketing itself as dedicated to reducing greenhouse gas emissions while continuing to make profits from coal and petroleum.

159. **Greenwashing.** Refers to the way companies and businesses involved in mining, especially coal, try and disguise how environmentally destructive they are by pretending to be concerned about lessoning the impact of man-made global warming.

160. **Grievance culture.** Instead of individuals and groups embracing responsibility and personal agency, where they have control and the ability to act, grievance culture promotes the belief disadvantage stems from the structural nature of Western societies that are condemned as racist, sexist, exploitive and transphobic.

161. **Grievance studies.** As a result of the cultural-left's long march and the impact of neo-Marxist inspired critical theory and postmodernism universities have long since abandoned the concept of a liberal education. University courses now include: feminist, post-colonial, neo-Marxist, queer and transgender studies where what students learn is deconstructed and critiqued in terms of power relationships and the evils of Western civilisation.

162. **Guides by the side.** See facilitators.

163. **Halo bias.** Involves having a favourable and positive view of someone based on an initial impression. Much like affinity bias, halo bias is an example of unconscious bias prevalent in Western societies where privileged elites favour one another and stigmatise and marginalise the "other".

164. **Hate speech/hate crime.** The New South Wales Parliament describes hate speech as publicly threatening or inciting violence on the grounds of protected attributes such as race, religious

affiliation, sexual orientation, gender identity and intersex or HIV/AIDS status. At the Australian commonwealth level, under 18c of the Racial Discrimination Act, hate speech refers to "anything that is reasonably likely in all the circumstances to offend, insult, humiliate or intimidate on the grounds of race". Such is the force of the political correctness movement and identity politics that anyone who infringes the protected attributes is liable to be fined, imprisoned or made to suffer the consequences of what can be a lengthy and expensive legal process.

In Tasmania a transgender activist lodged a complaint with the Human Rights Commission against the Catholic Archbishop Julian Porteous for circulating a booklet detailing the Church's views about marriage. In Queensland three students underwent a lengthy, expensive and very public ordeal for complaining about not being able to use a computer centre set aside for indigenous students. The example of the conservative newspaper columnist Andrew Bolt being convicted for questioning the veracity of individuals claiming Aboriginal heritage also demonstrates how accusing people of so-called hate speech is being used to curtail free speech and enforce group think.

165. **Health care hesitancy.** Monica Doumit in *The Catholic Weekly* cites secular critics arguing against freedom of religion on the basis to do otherwise leads to health care hesitancy. A situation where, if Christian hospitals, doctors

and health care workers remained true to their faith, people apparently would be afraid that they would be subjected to derogatory comments in health care service and so avoid medical care. (*The Catholic Weekly*, 30 January 2022).

166. **Health equity.** The *Guide to Language, Narrative and Concepts* published by the American Medical Association and the Association of American Medical Colleges Centre for Health, instead of referring to the Hippocratic Oath telling doctors their primary duty is to care for their patients and to do no harm, prioritises "health equity"; described as a scholarly domain and a central issue in medicine. As such the doctor's duty is "to address all areas of marginalization and inequity due to sexism, class oppression, homophobia, xenophobia and ableism". The first step is to understand the prevalence of ill health, disease and sickness is "directly related, indeed produced and reinforced by inequities in other parts of society".

167. **Hegemony.** What appears natural or normal is often not the case and hegemony refers to how those in control of capitalist society are able to dominate others by conditioning them to accept their inferior and less privileged position. This can be achieved either by economic and political control or more subtly through controlling what happens in education, the marketplace and the media. (See also agitprop and false consciousness.) In order to win the revolution the Italian

Marxist Antonio Gramsci argued it was vital that activists took control of education to counter the hegemonic influence exerted by the state.

168. **Heteronormative equivalency.** The Sydney gender activist Jessica Merritt argues those in the gay/lesbian community advocating same-sex marriage are guilty of imposing "heteronormative equivalency" on the LGBTIQ+ community. A situation where a conservative mainstream institution is seen as more authentic than the existing relationship between gay and lesbian couples.

169. **Heteronormativity.** The 'OMG My Friend's Queer' booklet associated with the Safe Schools program defines this as the "assumption that everyone is straight". Although approximately 98% of Australians according to one national survey self-identify as male or female LGBTIQ+ advocates argue it is wrong to assume that being heterosexual is normal. The University of Illinois Library describes heteronormativity as "a form of power and control that applies pressure to both straight and gay individuals through institutional arrangements and accepted social norms".

170. **Heterosexism.** The Monash "Inclusive Language Guide", under Glossary, describes this as referring to "the individual, group or institutional norms and behaviours that result from the assumption that all people are heterosexual, assuming heterosexuality is inherently normal or superior".

171. **Heterosexuality.** When discussing the concept of compulsory heterosexuality the *encyclopedia of glbtq culture* defines this as "the assumption that women and men are innately attracted to each other emotionally and sexually and that heterosexuality is normal and universal". Societies that endorse the love between a woman and a man are condemned because the "institutionalization of heterosexuality in our society leads to an institutionalized inequality of power".

Ignored is that if humanity is to survive men and women need to be attracted to one another for the purpose of procreation. Also ignored is the reality that the overwhelming majority of babies are either born female (XX chromosomes) or male (XY).

172. **Homophobia.** The Safe Schools material defines this as the "fear, hatred or ignorance towards same sex attracted people and people who are attracted to more than one gender. Homophobia usually leads to discrimination or abuse, like using the phrase 'that's so gay'". The definition is a broad one and, as a result, those who are heteronormative and defend marriage as between a woman and a man are often attacked as homophobic. After the tennis legend Margaret Court argued against same sex marriage and transgenderism another tennis legend Martina Navratilova condemned her as "a racist and a homophobe".

173. **Horizontally challenged.** Instead of being labelled fat or overweight such individuals are described as horizontally

challenged. Alternatives include "differently sized" and having "an alternative body image". (See also fat shaming.)

174. **House-keeping.** The University of Washington's "Inclusive Language Guide" warns against using the expression as it "carries a fraught history and connotation of women's traditional domestic role as housekeepers". As such it reinforces the way women are unjustly treated in what is a male dominated, patriarchal society.

175. **Humanewashing.** The animal activist group Direct Action Everywhere describes this as "a systematic effort to disguise brutal violence against animals as responsible or compassionate".

176. **Ideology.** Roger Scruton in *Culture Counts*, when discussing the meaning of ideology and drawing on Karl Marx, defines ideology as "a collection of ideas that have no authority in themselves but which disguise and mystify the social reality". Terry Eagleton in *Literary Theory* describes ideology as "the ways in which what we say and believe connects with the power-structure and power relations of the society we live in". Radical second and third wave feminists argue that young girls and women are conditioned by a patriarchal, misogynist ideology to accept their inferior roles as wives and mothers.

177. **Ideological state apparatus.** Made famous by Louis Althusser the expression refers to the way capitalist economies maintain power and can reproduce themselves. Althusser differentiates between a repressive state apparatus and an ideological one; the second involves institutions associated with religion, the education system, family, and political, legal and cultural systems. Taken together such institutions enforce the ruling ideology by conditioning citizens to accept as natural or beneficial what is oppressive and exploitive.

178. **Identity history.** Australia's Stuart Macintyre in *The History Wars* details the rise of what he describes as "history from below" during the 1960s and 1970s; a time when history teaching began to focus on "social movements formed around sexuality, race and ethnicity". Instead of dealing with mainstream events, movements and individuals Macintyre argues minority groups assumed centre stage; leading to a situation where "identity history has been practised widely over the last two decades".

179. **Identity Politics.** The British politician Michael Gove associates the emergence of identity politics with the cultural-revolution of the late '60s and early '70s and the influence of critical theory. Instead of individuals being part of a broader community with common interests they identify as one of the numerous victim groups oppressed and marginalised

by capitalism and Western civilisation. The argument that LGBTIQ+ people, people of colour and women deserve positive discrimination simply because of their unique character is an example of identity politics. Instead of being judged according to their character, as Martin Luther King Jr argued in his "I have a dream" speech, such individuals portray themselves as victims because of their religion, race, gender, class or sexuality.

180. **Incels.** Short for "involuntary celibate", incels refers to those men who share in common an inability to attract and be comfortable with women. The *Urban Dictionary* describes incels as "a person (usually male) who has a horrible personality and treats women like sexual objects and thinks his lack of a sex life comes from being 'ugly' when it's really just his blatant sexism and terrible attitude".

181. **Internalised colonialism.** A "Social Justice Report 2011" by the Australian Human Rights Commission lists internalised colonialism as a synonym for lateral violence. Instead of individual Aborigines being blamed for violence, bullying, back-stabbing and harassment their "behaviour is often the result of disadvantage, discrimination and oppression" arising from colonialism and unfair discrimination.

182. **Intersectionality.** A paper delivered at the 22nd International Summit on Violence, Abuse and Trauma held

in California describes intersectionality as "overlapping or intersecting social identities and related systems of oppression, domination and/or discrimination". Identities that can intersect include "gender, race, social class, ethnicity, nationality, sexual orientation, religion, age, mental disability, physical disability, mental illness and physical illness, etc". The *Urban Dictionary* defines intersectionality as "an all-you-can-eat buffet of mental illnesses and victim statuses". An example of intersectionality is an individual who is vertically challenged, queer, non-white and experiencing mental and physical disabilities.

The international Women's Development Agency describes "Intersectionality" as "acknowledging the interplay between gender and other forms of discrimination, like race, age, class, socioeconomic status, physical or mental ability, gender or sexual identity, religion, or ethnicity". For example, the barriers faced by a middle-class woman living in Melbourne are not the same as those of a queer woman living in rural Fiji.

183. **Institutional racism.** London's Royal Court theatre describes institutional racism as a form of racism either covertly or overtly "resides in the policies, procedures, operation and culture of public and private institutions – reinforcing individual prejudices and being reinforced by them in return whether conscious or unconscious".

184. **Islamophobic.** Mehmet Ozaip on *The Conversation* website defines Islamophobia as a special form of racism revealing "indiscriminate negative attitudes or emotions directed at Islam and Muslims. An Islamophobic incident is any act comprising of abusive hatred, vilification and violence inflicted on Muslims going about their daily lives". Based on this definition anyone who criticises the Koran for advocating a jihad against the West or for sanctioning the mistreatment of women is islamophobic. One example is the Somalian Muslim female Ayaan Hirsi Ali who is condemned as an islamophobe for daring to argue in her book *Heretic* that "Islam is not a religion of peace".

185. **In bed with a wog.** An obsolete expression once used to describe being in bed because of catching a cold or the flu. Now considered an example of unconscious racism as "wog" is a description that demeans and offends Italians as well as people from Asia (otherwise known as Worthy Oriental Gentlemen).

186. **Intersex.** The Monash University "Inclusive Language Guide" defines intersex as including "a variety of biological conditions; intersex people are born with physical, hormonal or genetic features that are neither wholly female nor wholly male; or a combination of female and male; or neither female nor male".

187. **Intersexphobia/Interphobia.** The OECD report "LGBTI in OECD Countries" defines this as Fear of,

discrimination against, or hatred of intersex people. The word "intersexphobia" was coined by the Organisation Intersex International (OII), while the term "interphobia" was introduced by Cary Gabriel Costello, an intersex trans-male professor of sociology at the University of Wisconsin, Milwaukee.

188. **Jazz hands.** According to the UK *The Daily Mail* the student union at the University of Manchester is asking students to show appreciation and enjoyment by Jazz hands as the loud and intrusive noise and movement caused by clapping might trigger anxiety and alarm.

189. **Judeo-Christianity.** While Pope Francis uses the expression to stress the close association between the Jewish and Christian faiths the Australian historian Tony Taylor describes Judeo-Christianity as a "fabricated myth". A myth used by conservatives when arguing the Old and New Testaments are necessary to any understanding of what constitutes Western civilisation.

190. **Karen.** A pejorative word to describe a middle-aged, well-off, typically blond women who parades her entitlement by complaining against even the smallest attempt to promote greater equity, diversity and social justice.

191. **Keep it up.** An expression once widely used to motivate and encourage but is now considered politically incorrect

as it is considered phallocentric and misogynist as it appears to privilege the sex act from a person with a penis (male) perspective.

192. **Knowledge navigators.** See digital natives.

193. **Lawfare.** John Steenhof, a Canberra-based lawyer and human rights activist, defines lawfare as "the process of attempting to coerce or punish a person's actions through litigation". Lawfare is often used by cultural-left activists to punish and silence those advocating politically incorrect ideas, beliefs and convictions.

194. **Lateral violence.** The Native Women's Association of Canada defines lateral violence, whether at home, at work or in the community, as abuse, intimidation and violence directed at one's own "gender, culture, sexuality and profession". Instead of acknowledging individual responsibility and agency the guide argues lateral violence is "a learned behaviour as a result of colonialism and patriarchal methods of governing and developing a society". If only Canadian aboriginals had been able to practice "their traditional teachings" there would be no violence and all would be well.

195. **Lesbophobia.** Preferred by those who argue the word "homophobia" is unacceptable as using the prefix "homo" privileges men and is guilty of phallocentrism. Lesbophobia involves an irrational and unjustified prejudice against lesbians.

196. **LGBTIQ+.** An acronym used to describe Lesbian, Gay, Bisexual, Transgender, Intersex, Queer and "plus" people. In the journal *English in Australia* (Vol. 53. No. 2) the editors explain using the symbol + acknowledges "these bounded labels are fluid and not exhaustive; they do not capture the complexities of time and place. It also works to include the other/future non-conforming identities".

197. **LGBTQA+.** Such is the fluid and indeterminant nature of gender theory that the acronyms keep changing. One of the more recent abbreviations is LGBTQA+ standing for lesbian, gay, bisexual, trans, queer/questioning, asexual with a + (plus) added for those wishing to self-identify with an unlimited range of other gender descriptions. On the Bustle media website the statement is made: "The spectrum of gender and sexuality is an endlessly diverse one, and adding the "QA+" acknowledges not just queer/questioning and asexual people (the Q and the A, respectively), but any other identity a person might have (the +). It's a wonderfully positive step forward for inclusion, as it serves to educate the public and counter the belief that heterosexuality is the norm to which everything else should be compared".

198. **LINO.** Liberals in name only is an Australian political expression like the American RINO – Republicans in name only. It refers to those in the Liberal Party who instead of supporting conservative beliefs and values argue for centre left polices associated with the Australian Labor Party.

199. **Literature.** An arcane and elitist category of texts usually referring to those plays, poems, short stories and novels that have something lasting and profound to say about human nature and the world in which we live. Terry Eagleton in *Literary Theory* an Introduction details the impact of theory and notes we cannot assume that what is "currently termed 'literature' will always and everywhere be the most important focus of attention". Eagleton goes as far as suggesting "Anything can be literature, and anything that can be regarded unalterably and unquestionably literature – Shakespeare for example – can cease being literature".

The politically correct alternative "texts" is now preferred, defined by the Australian national curriculum as anything communicated in "written, spoken, visual, multimodal, and in print or digital/online forms. Multimodal texts combine language with other means of communication such as visual images, soundtrack or spoken words, as in film or computer presentation media".

200. **Lizard brain.** Refers to the primitive side of the brain that deals with basic instincts including fight or flight, eating, sleeping and fornication. Woke activists often characterise the unwoke as having lizard brains because they are driven by anger and hatred towards the other.

201. **Lockdown denier.** The British newspaper columnist Dan Hodges, when debating with Peter Hitchens, uses the expression

lockdown denier to describe those opposed to the COVID-19 lockdown (aired on UK's Talk Radio's *Head to Head*).

202. **Love media.** The Sky News commentator Chris Kenny refers to "love media" when describing the cultural-left inclined media committed to woke ideology in areas such global warming, gender and feminist theories plus the evils of Western civilisation and capitalist society.

203. **MAGA.** An acronym standing for Make America Great Again and associated with President Trump and his supporters. Jussie Smollett, a black gay American actor who staged a fake episode of hate crime, had one of the attackers cry: "This is MAGA country". The fact that mainstream media was so quick to describe the incident as true and an example of white racism is an example of politically correct fake news (otherwise known as agitprop).

204. **Male.** A binary, heteronormative description that privileges and normalises masculinity to the exclusion of other more liberating and authentic forms of LGBTIQ+ gender and sexuality.

205. **Male assigned at birth.** Used to describe an individual's birth-sex on the basis, instead of being biologically determined, that traditional binary sex categories are restrictive social constructs imposed on innocent and

unsuspecting babies by a heteronormative, transphobic society (also known as male bodied).

206. **Male colonisation.** The Australian journalist Nikki Gemmell condemns the publishers Allen and Unwin for choosing a male journalist to write about the #MeToo movement as an example of "men colonising women's domains". Gemmell describes the #MeToo movement as "courageous, fraught, intensely female" and argues that asking a man to write about the issue is simply another example of "structural sexism" where men are privileged and given preferential treatment over women.

207. **Male, Pale and Stale.** A description employed by the woke, especially third wave feminists to condemn those older, white males who refuse to endorse woke ideology and group think. (See also RWNJ.)

208. **Man box.** A journalist at The Fairfax Press, Anna Prytz, describes a man box as when men are hemmed in and constrained because they believe "that men should be unemotional, hyper-sexual, physically tough, stoic and in control". Men being brave, sexually active, physically strong and in control of their emotions is politically incorrect as such attributes are binary in nature and ignore the need for men to be more in touch with their feminine and LGBTIQ+ side. (See also toxic masculinity.)

209. **Manhole.** A description that reinforces male dominance. Alternatives include "personnel access structure", "femhole" or "utility hole". The Berkeley City Council in California mandates in its municipal code that "manhole" be replaced by "maintenance hole".

210. **Manshaming.** Describes the process of unfairly attacking and criticising men and making them feel guilty because they are men – usually, but not always, involves second and third wave feminists. School programs dealing with domestic violence like Respectful Relationships present men as violent and dangerous without any acknowledgement that not all men are guilty. The Gillette video "Is this the best a man can get?" has also been criticised for presenting a biased and one-sided view of men.

In response to the appalling and distressing death of Courtney Herron in Melbourne the Assistant Commissioner of Police Luke Cornelius describes all men as guilty. Even though the alleged psychotic male responsible acted alone and it was late at night in an isolated, dark park on being interviewed Cornelius argues "The key point is (that) this is men's behaviour, it's not about women's behaviour".

211. **Mansplaining.** Refers to those men who treat women as unintelligent and incapable of understanding by being condescending and patronising. The University of Adelaide was recently criticised for a billboard showing a man seated

surrounded by a number of female students passively listening while he held centre stage talking.

212. **Mansplaying.** Refers to the way men and boys maximise their seating space on public transport by sitting with their legs open as wide as possible. Also seen by radical feminists as an unwarranted and offensive display of male dominance and of phallocentrism.

213. **Manterruptions.** Described as a man continually interrupting a woman by dominating the conversation and talking over her.

214. **MAPS.** Refers to minor attracted people (otherwise known as paedophiles). Allyn Walker, the author of *A Long dark Shadow: Minor-Attracted People and Their Pursuit of Dignity*, argues the term is less stigmatising and offensive to those attracted to children.

215. **Marriage.** Historically and across cultures marriage has been defined as the union of a woman and a man for the purpose of procreation and the survival of the species. Cultural-left critics, on the other hand, argue marriage is a relationship that institutionalises the oppression and mistreatment of women. Marriage, instead of being reciprocal is an institution invented by patriarchal societies for the benefit of men. Radical feminists consider sex within marriage as a form of exploitation except if you are gay,

lesbian, trans, intersex or queer where getting married is a form of liberation that publicly validates gayness/queerness.

As argued by Neel Burton in *Psychology Today* "On the marriage market, women are made to feel like low value, perishable goods. To find a taker, whether for marriage or just for sex, they need, much more than men, to conform to sexist, ageist, and racist stereotypes, and do appalling things such as wear makeup and high heels, which become the visible symbols of their oppression". Some feminists equate marriage with prostitution on the basis that both involve subjugation and sexual exploitation by men in what is a phallocentric, male dominated society.

216. **Meme.** *The Oxford Dictionary* defines a meme as "An element of a culture or system of behaviour passed from one individual to another by imitation or other non-genetic means". For example, as a result of watching the film *Birdbox* thousands around the world competed to wear blindfolds in challenging situations. Such was the danger that Netflix issued a statement "Can't believe I have to say this, but: PLEASE DO NOT HURT YOURSELVES WITH THIS BIRD BOX CHALLENGE. We don't know how this started, and we appreciate the love, but Boy and Girl have just one wish for 2019 and it is that you not end up in the hospital due to memes".

217. **#MeToo movement.** An international movement against sexual assault and harassment initially sparked by the Harvey Weinstein scandal but that now provides a world-wide platform to identify and punish men guilty of such offenses. While applauded in Hollywood as justifiable the French actress Catherine Deneuve signed an open letter with 99 other women in criticising the #MeToo movement for being puritanical and guilty of treating women as passive and always the victim in their relationships with men.

218. **#MenToo.** The Australian author Bettina Arndt in her book *#MenToo* argues that in the West we are living in an anti-male society where men are demonised and treated unfairly by radical feminists and gender warriors. In areas like family divorce, domestic violence and youth suicide Arndt argues men's rights are considered secondary to those of women.

219. **Microaggression.** In addition to obvious forms of aggression and victimisation microaggression refers to those politically incorrect acts, while never intending to be offensive, that are calculated to insult oppressed individuals and groups. One example that went viral around the internet is when the then Australian Leader of the Opposition Julia Gillard in parliament condemned Prime Minister Tony Abbott as hostile to women for looking at his watch while she was giving a long-winded speech.

220. **Misandry.** Involves unfairly criticising or condemning men and boys by presenting a stereotype that paints males as misogynist, sexist, violent and exploitive.

221. **Misgendering.** In the words of a language guide prepared by the Australian Defence Force Academy misgendering involves incorrectly addressing LGBTIQ+ personnel by using heteronormative pronouns like "he" or "she" when such personnel self-identify as the opposing gender. The guide states using language that fails to respect the gender identity of those being addressed "can have a significant effect on transgender individuals as it is often an expression of a lack of understanding of acceptance of that person's identity". A famous Australian example involves Major Gaynor Sr being warned about continuing to use a male pronoun when addressing a fellow officer who transitioned to become a woman (now known as Cate McGregor).

222. **Misspeaking.** The description used when you suddenly realise what you have said or are halfway through saying is politically incorrect and you have entered the killing zone. The British Labour politician Angela Smith when talking about non-white people described them as having a "funny tin" before stopping and apologising for misspeaking. The assumption is she was about to say "tint" or "tinge".

223. **Motherhood.** An exploitive and heteronormative concept imposed by patriarchal societies to restrict women to

childbearing and remaining dependent on men. Andrea O'Reilly in *Outlaw(ing) Motherhood: A Theory and Politic of Maternal Empowerment for the Twenty-First Century* describes motherhood as an example of "gender essentialism" that disempowers and oppresses women and argues "Only by unearthing and severing the ideological underpinning of patriarchal motherhood, gender essentialism, can we develop a politic of maternal empowerment and a practice of outlaw motherhood for the twenty-first century".

224. **Misogynist.** A term used to describe men who exhibit and demonstrate a hostility and dislike towards women. Berit Brogaard in *Psychology Today* argues misogyny is often unconscious and that "Women haters (unconsciously) get off on treating women badly. Every time they can put down a woman or hurt her feelings, they unconsciously feel good because deep down in their hidden brain, their bad behavior is rewarded with a dose of the pleasure chemical dopamine —which makes them want to repeat the behaviour again and again".

225. **Misogyny.** Defined as the hatred, dislike mistrust or prejudice that men feel towards women. According to the Victorian Government's Respectful Relationships material men are inherently violent towards women on the basis that one of the principal causes of violence against women is "a traditional view about gender roles and relationships". The argument is put that "men who are hostile towards women's

non-conformity to gender roles and to challenges to male authority have a particular tendency towards violence". Ignored is that other significant causes of domestic violence include poverty and drug and alcohol abuse.

226. **Misogynoir.** Attributed to the black, queer, feminist scholar Moya Bailey this refers to a form of abuse directed at black women that stems from the intersectionality of misogyny and racism. The *Herald Sun* cartoonist Mark Knight's depiction of Serena Williams abusing the umpire and smashing her tennis racket during the US Open Tennis final is politically incorrect as it is guilty, supposedly, of presenting Williams as a black, angry woman.

227. **Mother's Day.** See Father's Day.

228. **Multiculturalism.** Multiculturalism, unlike integration, involves treating all cultures as equal except for Western culture that is seen as Eurocentric, oppressive and guilty of "whiteness". The Australian *Civics and Citizenship* curriculum describes Australia as a "diverse and dynamic society" and "and a "secular nation with a multi-cultural and multi-faith society".

229. **Nanny state.** Refers to governments interfering and taking control of people's lives based on the premise that citizens are incapable of looking after themselves and being responsible. Because of political correctness governments have become

even more protective on the assumption that the state knows best and must be the final arbiter. One Australian example relates to aviation firefighters not being able to use ladders over 2 metres high for safety reasons. Another example involves local governments banning monkey bars in playgrounds because they put children at risk and schools stopping children doing cartwheels in the playground.

230. **Nativity scenes.** Once a widely accepted way to celebrate Christmas and the birth of Christ but now see as divisive and unacceptable as Australia is a multi-faith, multi-cultural, multi-ethnic society. It is wrong to privilege what is a Eurocentric, Christian event as all cultures and all religions (except for Christianity) deserve equal treatment.

231. **Neurotypical.** The offence of casting a healthy actor in the role of a character experiencing autism. At the 78th Globe awards the Australian songwriter Sia committed the offence in her nominated film *Music*. (See also cultural appropriation.)

232. **Nip in the air.** An expression once used to describe feeling cold but now considered politically incorrect as it is offensive to those of Japanese origin. Alternatives include "a chill in the air" and "being physically inconvenienced because of suboptimal temperature".

233. **No-platforming.** Refers to the practice of denying politically incorrect speakers the right to speak publicly at events because

their views are deemed offensive and unacceptable. The feminist Germaine Greer was no platformed in the UK at a university event because she argues a man who transitions to become a woman can never be a woman. The Australian Bettina Arndt also faces opposition when trying to talk at universities because she argues men are discriminated against in favour of women in areas like divorce proceedings and domestic violence. Arndt also argues the prevalence of female students being sexually harassed on university campuses is overstated.

234. **Non-animalist language.** The People for the Ethical Treatment of Animals (PETA) condemns language that oppresses and commodifies animals and produces resources for schools to help children be more caring and sensitive. Examples include:

Politically incorrect	**Non-animalist**
Kill two birds with one stone	Feed two birds with one stone
Let the cat out of the bag	Spill the beans
Take the bull by the horns	Take the flower by the thorns
Be a guinea pig	Be a test tube
Bring home the bacon	Bring home the bagels
More than one way to skin a cat	More than one way to skin a potato

235. **Non-disabled person.** In order not to offend people with a disability the University of Washington's Inclusive Language Guide argues against using words like "normal" and "healthy".

Disabled people are in fact "equally healthy" and the approved alternatives include non-disabled person, neurotypical person and person without disabilities.

236. **Non-gender normative/non-heteronormative.** According to a paper published in *English in Australia* (Vol.53. No.2) titled "Textual Constraints: Queering the Senior English Text List in the Australian Curriculum" the overwhelming majority of selected texts for senior school students deal with heteronormative, binary characters, themes and relationships. The paper argues to rectify the imbalance there must be more texts embracing a definition of gender and sexuality that is fluid and dynamic. Texts that are non-gender normative and non-heteronormative.

237. **Offendarati.** Aboriginal academic at the Australian Catholic University Anthony Dillion sources the expression to the Australian cartoonist Bill Leak when referring to woke activists promoting victimhood and always willing to take offense.

238. **Ooga booga.** The Australian television children's show *Bluey* has been criticised for using the expression "ooga booga". While the origins of the expression are unclear one reference refers to primitive tribes and the language they use, as in: "It's the ooga booga tribe" – "What are they saying?" – "I don't know but it sounds like 'Ooga booga'".

In *The Sydney Morning Herald* Victoria Morgan, a senior editor for *The Macquarie Dictionary* is quoted as saying "the term seems to have been popularised via Hollywood films in the 1930s and 1940s. At that time you had movies like *Tarzan* and *King Kong*. A lot of the actors from traditional cultures are represented extremely tribally, running around with spears and this sort of unintelligible language saying, 'ooga booga'. It's considered extremely derogatory. We see it in reference to Polynesian cultures, Indigenous Australians (and) Maori".

239. **Oppositional defiance disorder.** It's no longer acceptable for teachers to label students as disruptive or to punish them for offensive behaviour. Such students are suffering from Oppositional Defiance Disorder and are not responsible for their actions. Instead of being punished or reprimanded such students are entitled to additional resources and a personalised curriculum to ensure they are treated fairly, not discriminated against and given the opportunity to reach their full potential.

240. **Oppositional sexism.** According to the Diversity and Inclusion Glossary this refers to the belief femininity and masculinity are rigid and exclusive categories.

241. **Orientalism.** Roger Scruton attributes this expression to Edward Said and describes it as denoting the West's attitude to the Middle East. An attitude that suggests a "denigrating and patronizing attitude towards eastern civilizations" and that portrays the Middle East as "a world of wan indifference and vaporous intoxication".

242. **Over-smiling.** The American author Robin DiAngelo in *Nice Racism* describes white smiling as an example of unintended racism displayed when encountering a black person. She writes "Over-smiling allows white people to mask an anti-blackness that is fundamental to our very existence as white". Cited in Matthew Knott's "Colour Code" published in *The Saturday Age*, Good Weekend, 19 February 2022.

243. **Pandemic porn.** While the expression refers to the dramatic increase in viewing pornographic websites during COVID-19 it also refers to the way the mainstream media has exaggerated the dangers of the virus. Since the arrival of the virus in the West early 2020, every day the media has portrayed the virus as a deadly beast where all are vulnerable unless there is draconian government intervention.

244. **Pansexual.** The *Them* website defines pansexual as "someone who is attracted to people of all genders – not just cisgender and transgender men and women, but nonbinary people, gender-nonconforming people, and anyone whose genders fall outside of the gender binary, or beyond traditional definitions of what it means to be a 'man' or 'woman'". An extreme example of someone who is pansexual is Calum Jones who describes himself as "a heteroflexible pansexual solo polyamorous relationship anarchist".

245. **Partner.** A term once used to describe those working together in business or commerce but now the preferred gender-neutral term for those who are married or living in a long-term relationship.

246. **Patriarchal.** Feminists argue that Western society is ruled by men who subjugate and dominate women. There is no equality between the sexes as institutions like marriage force women to be chattels exploited by men. The Australian feminist Dale Spender sees patriarchy in every aspect and structure of society, a situation where "I am using patriarchy in all of these senses; I am using it as in inclusive term to encompass a sex-class system, and a symbolic system which supports male supremacist social arrangements. That is why I see patriarchy everywhere; there is no aspect of our lives, that I know of, which is outside patriarchy". The language we use is not immune and in "Man Made Society", Spender argues "Every aspect of the language from its structure to the conditions of its use must be scrutinised if we are to detect both the blatant and the subtle means by which the edifice of male supremacy has been assembled".

247. **Perception bias.** The American diversity consultant Stacey Gordon describes this as the tendency to form stereotypes and assumptions about certain groups that makes it difficult to make an objective judgement about the individual members of such groups. Examples include men who are male, pale and stale being biased against a particular woman because they are misogynists.

248. **People with a penis.** Descriptions such as boys and men, given the rise of neo-Marxist inspired gender theory and transgenderism, are now cancelled as they reinforce a binary, one-dimensional and oppressive view of sexuality.

249. **Performance activism.** Instead of being sincere and fully committed to woke issues and causes those guilty of performance activism only act to impress others and present themselves in the best light.

250. **Pets.** *The Journal of Animal Ethics*, edited by Reverend Professor Andrew Linzey, argues the term "pets" is unacceptable as it demeans and commodifies animals. The alternative description is "companion animals" – otherwise known as "God's sentient creatures".

251. **Phallic teacher.** Lucinda McKnight from Deakin University refers to Phallacism as worshipping the phallus (penis) and describes the phallic teacher as "the empowered, high quality, tool-wielding teacher discursively created by a neoliberal educational regime". McKnight argues incorporating an evidence-based approach to teaching and using standardised tests to measure performance is guilty of preferencing "masculinist authority".

252. **Pink washing.** Employed by the LGBTIQ+ community to describe those corporations, businesses and politicians

who pretend to be friendly and supportive in order to appear progressive and non-binary while still being hetero-normative and guilty of homophobia and transphobia. (See also virtue signalling.)

253. **Politically correct coding.** Rudy Takala, who writes for Media ITE, reports Twitter is dedicated to making code more politically correct by removing offense language used by programmers. Takala quotes the Twitter webpage as arguing "At Twitter, the language we have been using in our code does not reflect our values as a company or represent the people we serve. We want to change that". Takala lists the words it intends to change include replacing "whitelist" with "allowlist", "blacklist" with "denylist", and "master/slave" with "leader/follower". Others include switching "grandfathered" out in favour of "legacy status", "gendered pronouns" such as "guys" with "folks", "people", or "you all", and "sanity check" with "quick check" or "confidence check".

254. **Post journalism.** Martin Gurri in New York's *City Journal* describes post journalism as involving a "pivot from a journalism of fact to a 'post-journalism' of opinion". Gurri, after referring to Andrey Mir's book *Postjournalism*, argues the traditional print media's falling advertising revenue, the impact of the new digital technologies and the arrival of President Trump required a new style of reporting. Its language aimed to commodify polarisation and threat. Young, woke journalists argued instead

of impartiality and balance the media had to be involved in an "explicit struggle against injustice".

255. **Postmodernism.** The *Stanford Encyclopedia of Philosophy* describes postmodernism as "a set of critical, strategic and rhetorical practices employing concepts such as difference, repetition, the trace, the simulacrum, and hyperreality to destabilize other concepts such as presence, identity, historical progress, epistemic certainty, and the univocity of meaning". There are no truths we can agree on because how we perceive and understand ourselves and our relationship to the wider world is relative and subjective. Except of course for the belief that postmodernism is the correct way to interpret and understand one's identity and one's place in the world.

Richard Tarnes describes postmodernism as the belief "that human knowledge is subjectively determined by a multitude of factors; that objective essences, or things-in-themselves, are neither accessible nor positable... The critical search for truth is constrained to be tolerant of ambiguity and pluralism, and its outcome will necessarily be knowledge that is relative and fallible rather than absolute or certain".

256. **Poststructuralism.** Similar to postmodernism, post-structuralism denies the referential quality of language, objectivity and the inherent meaning of texts. Terry Eagleton in *Literary Theory* makes the point "If meaning,

the signified, was a passing product of words or signifiers, always shifting and unstable, part-present and part-absent, how could there be any determinate truth or meaning at all?". Taken to its logical conclusion poststructuralism makes it impossible to engage in rational discussion and debate as arguments and opinions are incapable of being objectively tested or verified.

257. **Pansexual.** An individual who is neither Cisfemale nor Cismale but who enjoys being romantically and physically involved with individuals of all genders and sexes.

258. **Phallocentric.** Taken from the Greek "phallus" – meaning "penis" and "centric" meaning "centred on"; feminists argue that Western society is phallocentric in nature as men are privileged whereas women are treated as inferior and ripe for exploitation. Pointing a finger when making a statement or presenting an argument is an example of being phallocentric and the politically correct alternative for those who are woke is to hold out one's hand with the palm upwards.

259. **People of Colour (POC).** The diversity consulting organisation The Moxie Exchange describes POC as encompassing "all non-white people in order to emphasize the common experience of systemic racism" suffered by non-white people.

260. **Pregnant person.** According to Melbourne-based The Equality Institute it is unacceptable to use the description "pregnant women" as limiting childbirth to women is an unfair and discriminatory binary, heteronormative concept. The Institute recommends "try using the phrase 'Pregnant people' because people of all genders can fall pregnant". The Institute goes on to argue "Consider all people when using language – including trans and non-binary folk – and ensure that your language is inclusive of everyone, when talking about pregnancy or anything else. Language matters". The City of Berkeley in California also recommends using the description "pregnant employees" as opposed to "pregnant women" to recognise the importance of "non-binary gender inclusivity".

261. **Positive discrimination.** Based on the belief that as Western, capitalist societies systematically oppress and disadvantage marginalised groups the only solution is to positively discriminate in favour of victim groups and oppressed individuals to ensure equality of outcomes. Instead of relying on merit and ability the PC alternative it to mandate equal gender representation in areas like corporate boards and preselection for election to parliament.

262. **Post-colonial theory.** Drawing on Edward Said's book *Orientalism* this refers to the way Western imperial powers justify colonialism and the accompanying violence

and exploitation by describing it as a "civilising mission". Those cultures invaded are defined through Western eyes as inferior and described as uncivilised and representing the "the Other" to justify their mistreatment. Critics of Western countries guilty of imperialism rarely, if ever, mention the role Islam played in its invasion and subjugation of other countries and territories.

263. **Punching down.** The Australian comedian Diana Nguyen (*The Age*, 18 October 2020), when discussing mimicking her Vietnamese mother's accent, suggests "I would never do my mother's accent to have her laughed at. It's a question of representation. Asian cultures have been mocked a lot... When white people used Asian accents in the past, it was punching down". Punching down involves someone in a superior position because of race, status, class denigrating or making fun of someone considered as inferior. The *Urban Dictionary* describes punching down as "For someone of higher rank, power, status, and position to engage someone of much lesser and/or inferior rank, status, power, and position in debate and/or argument".

264. **Punching up.** Australian comedian Simon Hall (*The Age*, 18 October 2020), when discussing whether or not it is OK to mimic a foreign accent, argues "Who's performing the accent matters, as does the power dynamic between the performer and the performed: punching down is very

different to punching up". The implication being while it is wrong to mimic or make fun of those described as victims it is OK to belittle and satirise those individuals or groups considered elitist and privileged. The *Urban Dictionary* defines punching up as "Making jokes at the expense of someone who is of a higher level of power in terms of status or privilege".

265. **Queerbaiting.** Involves films and TV shows, in order to attract viewers, highlighting a scene where same-sex attracted characters are intimate. Often the scene is tokenistic.

266. **Queer Theory.** Drawing on the French academic and psychologist Foucault and in opposition to categories like "gay" and "lesbian", queer theory posits that gender and sexuality are social constructs and, as a result, resist any clear or definite definition. The *Stanford Encyclopedia of Philosophy*, under the heading Homosexuality, suggests "In contrast to gay or lesbian, 'queer,' it is argued, does not refer to an essence, whether of a sexual nature or not. Instead, it is purely relational, standing as an undefined term that gets its meaning precisely by being that which is outside of the norm, however that norm itself may be defined". The author goes on to quote David M. Halperin's definition "Queer is... whatever is at odds with the normal, the legitimate, the dominant. There is nothing to which it necessarily refers. It is an identity without an essence".

267. **Race baiting.** *The Cambridge Dictionary* describes this as "the act of intentionally encouraging racism or anger about issues relating to race, often to get a political advantage". Conservative politicians arguing that violence within Black communities is often instigated by other blacks, even though it's true, are guilty of race baiting. (See also dog whistling.)

268. **Racial capitalism.** Drawing on the work of Cedric J. Robinson and his book *Black Marxism: The Making of the Black Radical Tradition,* Black Lives Matter activists argue capitalism is inherently racist and exploitive proven by the European and American slave trade.

269. **Race shifters.** The Canadian journalist Susan O'Donnell describes race shifters as "white people with no or a small amount of Indigenous ancestry who identify as Indigenous" ('Race-shifters; white people who identify as Indigenous'. NB Media Co-op, 22 November 2019). O'Donnell suggests race shifters fail to qualify as being indigenous according to a Supreme Court decision describing Indigenous people as those who self-identify, have an ancestral connection to the Indigenous community and are accepted by that community.

270. **Repressive tolerance.** One of the leading thinkers contributing to what has become known as cancel culture is Herbert Marcuse. In his essay "Repressive Tolerance", published in 1968, Marcuse argues no-one should be

allowed to question or doubt politically correct ideology or group think. Marcuse argues "... certain things cannot be said, certain ideas cannot be expressed, certain policies cannot be proposed, certain behavior cannot be permitted without making tolerance an instrument for the continuation of servitude".

271. **Reproductive coercion.** The Children by Choice website suggests reproductive coercion is just as widespread as rape and defines it as "an easy and effective and cowardly way of manipulating and controlling a woman by limiting her autonomy over her fertility and reproductive health and choices". Examples include men refusing to wear a condom during sexual intercourse and a man forcing a woman to become pregnant.

272. **Reverse ferret.** Refers to an organisation, politician or media celebrity reversing a previous held position, statement or belief without acknowledging the reversal.

273. **Reverse racism.** While some dislike the term (on the basis that racism is racism regardless of the target) the expression is used to denote an unfair prejudice and bias against a society's dominant race. An example of reverse racism is the assumption that white people are always privileged and are inherently prejudiced and incapable of accepting non-whites as equals. (See also whiteness and white supremacism.)

274. **Revenge feminism.** *The Australian*'s Janet Albrechtsen describes this extreme form of feminism as "one part of a larger body of grievance politics" influenced by postmodern theory that argues knowledge is a social construct and that all relationships are based on power and privilege. Western society is inherently misogynist and patriarchal and all men are guilty of oppressing and enslaving women.

275. **Right Wing Nut Job (RWNJ).** The Sky News commentator Chris Kenny refers to the woke expression as a criticism used by the cultural-left, PC brigade to denigrate and cancel those whose beliefs and ideas they refuse to accept. (See also male, pale and stale.)

276. **Sad fishing.** Given the prevalence of digital technologies and social networking sites young people, in particular, are using the new media when expressing feelings of loneliness and sadness. Sad fishing involves making public one's feelings and seeking a sympathetic response.

277. **Santa Claus.** A mythical figure used to delude children often with the hope of making them better behaved and to foster a commitment to materialism and consumerism. Rebecca English from the Queensland University of Technology argues "You shouldn't lie about Santa because you are encouraging your children, usually with made-up proof, to believe a morally ambiguous lie. I'm not alone in being devastated

learning of my parents' elaborate deceit about Santa, leaving me to wonder what other lies they had told".

278. **Safe Spaces.** Universities now have Safe Spaces to ensure there are havens for those oppressed by the Eurocentric, heteronormative, racist and sexist environment that prevails on campuses and in lectures and tutorials. University of Sydney Women's Officer Madeline Ward argues "safe spaces such as the on-campus Queer Space and the Wom*n's Room and ethno cultural room for 'people of colour' were necessary". Ward argues "I would say the queer and ethno spaces are vital because society is racist and homophobic" (*The Daily Telegraph* 9 August 2018).

The University of Southern Queensland's library policy on providing Safe Spaces states the university is committed to providing "a visible and inclusive safe area for staff and students who identify as lesbian, gay, bisexual, transgender, intersex or queer (LGBTIQ)".

279. **Safe Schools.** Roz Ward, who helped design the program, argues "Safe Schools Coalition is about supporting gender and sexual diversity, not about stopping bullying". She says it's about "sexual diversity, about same sex attraction, about being transgender, about being lesbian, gay, bisexual – say the words transgender, intersex". As with much of radical gender theory the ideology underpinning Safe Schools is heavily influenced by Marxism. Ward argues "only

Marxism provides the theory and practice of genuine human liberation" and "it will only be through a revitalised class struggle and revolutionary change that we can hope for the liberation of LGBTI people".

280. **Seahorse dad.** A description of a woman who undergoes gender transition to become a man but who still wants to give birth to a child. The journalist Freddy McConnell who was able to conceive is the subject of the film *Seahorse* and the film's director Jeanie Finlay argues it's OK for transman to give birth as "Lots of people want to have a baby... it's a natural thing".

281. **Sexist.** While the *Urban Dictionary* suggests anyone can be sexist, according to second and third wave feminists men are the worst offenders. Men are inherently sexist as they demean and objectify women as sexual objects and, unless properly conditioned, boys follow in their father's footsteps.

282. **Shadowbanning.** A form of censorship whereby a person's activity on a social networking site is curtailed or limited without their knowledge. In America Republican politicians and some conservative commentators accuse Twitter and Facebook of restricting access to their accounts by manipulating search engines and what is posted as to make it difficult, if not impossible, for them to be found by others using the internet.

283. **Sheila.** An offensive and outdated expression once used by Australian men to describe women. As in "she's a bonza sheila".

284. **Sensitivity tool kits.** See diversity tool kits.

285. **Sexuality.** Material associated with the Safe Schools program OMG I'm Queer argues that a person's sexuality is not determined by one's sex at birth rather it is fluid and subjective. "All people have their own sexuality. Whether that's straight, gay, queer, bisexual or something completely different; each person's sexuality applies only to them". The American College of Paediatricians, on the other hand, argue sexuality is binary in nature as "sexuality is an objective biological binary trait 'XY' and 'XX' are genetic markers of male and female, respectively – not genetic markers of a disorder. The norm for human design is to be conceived either male or female. Human sexuality is binary by design with the obvious purpose being the reproduction and flourishing of our species. This principle is self-evident".

286. **Short shaming.** Dan Kaufman in *The Age* complains about the prejudice displayed against short men in what is "a heightist world". Women prefer men who are tall, research shows short men are made to do more housework and expressions like "short changed" and "falling short" cause further harm.

287. **Sky fairy.** The *Urban Dictionary* describes the Sky fairy as the "name of any god, spirit or divine presence of which there is no evidence".

288. **Sky father.** See sky fairy.

289. **Slut shaming.** After announcing her intention not to re-contest her seat the federal Australian Labor Party member Emma Hussar stated that she was forced to resign because of "slut shaming". Leora Tanenbaum in the *HuffPost* describes this as "the experience of being labeled a sexually out-of-control girl or woman (a 'slut' or 'ho') and then being punished socially for possessing this identity. Slut-shaming is sexist because only girls and women are called to task for their sexuality, whether real or imagined; boys and men are congratulated for the exact same behavior. This is the essence of the sexual double standard boys will be boys, and girls will be sluts".

290. **Snowflakes.** Refers to recent generations of young people who lack confidence and resilience and who are easily offended and upset if confronted by what they consider politically incorrect. Trigger warnings and Safe Spaces exist to protect snowflakes as do politically correct concepts like identity politics and victimhood.

Young children are so anxious and concerned about missing out that a school in Sydney has banned birthday cards. A notice sent home to parents states, "At the request of parents, and in consultation with the school community,

Mosman Public School has asked that student birthday party invitations are not handed out during school hours due to the distress caused to students seen not to be invited".

291. **Space invader.** During an election campaign television debate where Prime Minister Scott Morrison walked towards and closed in on the then Leader of the Opposition Bill Shorten, Shorten complained Morrison was a "space invader". Space invaders are those who impose their physical presence on others denying them the right to private space and the need to feel safe and not threatened.

292. **Speciesism.** Animal rights activists argue that speciesism, similar to racism, sexism, homophobia and transphobia, involves those who see themselves as superior discriminating against and exploiting the'other' – in this case non-human sentient creatures. As stated by Germain Greer when hearing about the naturalist Steve Irwin being killed by a stingray "The animal world has finally taken its revenge".

293. **Spirit animal.** According to the University of Washington's Inclusive Language Guide, spirit animals are an important part of the belief system of some cultures and refer to a spirit that "helps guide or protect a person on a journey and whose characteristics that person shares or embodies". The guide states using the expression is offensive and an example of "cultural appropriation" is used by non-indigenous people.

294. **Spirit murdering.** The American blacktivist Bettina L. Love describes spirit murdering as follows: "Physical and psychological attacks on Black and Brown children's bodies and culture are more than just racist acts by misguided school educators; they are the spirit murdering of Black and Brown children". Woke activists argue schools, for example, are guilty of teaching white supremacism and that the curriculum must be decolonised and refocused to teach the unique strengths and benefits of non-white cultures and civilisations. In December 2020 a public debate erupted regarding CRT when teachers were told "The United States was built off the stolen labor of kidnapped and enslaved black people's work" and that teachers must forsake their whiteness and become "anti-racist educators".

295. **Stereotype threat.** The Australian National University's Gender Inclusive Handbook defines this as "reminding students of negative intellectual stereotypes associated with their category of identity. This 'reminder' can be communicated verbally and through academic materials, and it can occur to students who identify with a visible, numeric minority within the student body". An example of stereotype threat is teaching heteronormative literary works like Austen's *Pride and Prejudice* or racist novels including *Huckleberry Finn*.

296. **Structural racism.** Keith Lawrence and Terry Keleher in their essay "Structural Racism" describe it as "the normalization and legitimization of an array of dynamics

– historical, cultural, institutional and interpersonal – that routinely advantage whites while producing cumulative and chronic adverse outcomes for people of color. It is a system of hierarchy and inequity, primarily characterized by white supremacy...”

The UK Labor Politician Clive Lewis when interviewed on Sky News UK argues Meghan Markle, the former Duchess of Sussex, is a victim of structural racism when stating “We see it with Meghan Markle and the way she’s been treated in the media. We know this is a reality of the 21st century still after 400 years of racism”.

297. **Structural sexism.** Drawing on critical theory the argument is that even though women might be comfortable with their roles in society and feel they are treated fairly; the reality is society is inherently sexist and oppressive. The way society is structured, especially institutions like the family, education and work, conditions women to accept an inferior role while men dominate.

The Marxist inspired feminist Shulamith Firestone argues that the only way for women to achieve true freedom and equality is to radically reshape society by making men redundant. She writes in *The Dialectic Of Sex* “The end goal of the feminist revolution must be, unlike that of the first feminist movement, not just the elimination of male privilege but of the sex distinction itself, genital differences between human beings would no longer matter culturally”.

298. **SWERF (Sex-work exclusionary radical feminist).**

Refers to those feminists opposed to the sex industry as prostitution involves women being commodified and treated as sexual objects by men.

299. **Systematic oppression.** Based on Marxist concepts like hegemony and the ideological state apparatus the belief is that capitalist, Western societies are inherently inequitable and oppressive.

300. **TERF (Trans exclusionary radical feminist).** Described as a Ciswoman who intentionally offends transpeople by arguing that gender and sexuality are binary and that a man cannot transition to becoming a woman. In the English town of Macclesfield a transperson after being confronted by a women with a t-shirt with the words "Women: noun adult human female" argued "When you're trying to relax in your fave pub and there is a TERF wearing an anti-trans T-shirt... it's disgusting and I'm so upset by it".

301. **TCE.** Refers to Traditional Cultural Expression. Brigitte Vezina in "Curbing Cultural Appropriation in the Fashion Industry" criticises those in the West's fashion industry guilty of cultural appropriation by copying the designs and fabrics associated with non-white cultures. Examples include the American company Urban Outfitters producing clothing based on Navajo Nation motifs and designs and a French designer copying a traditional blouse worn by the

Mixe people – an Indigenous Mexican community. Vezina argues traditional cultural expression should be protected by enforcing intellectual property rights.

302. **The missus.** A misogynist and patriarchal expression used by husbands to describe their wives. Equally as offensive are descriptions like "she who must be obeyed" and the "better half". Wendy Tuohy in *The Age* argues a man using the expression treats his wife as a "person of lower status, over whom I have power and control, and whose opinions matter less than mine".

303. **The Long March.** Roger Kimball in his book *The Long March* attributes the phrase to German New Leftist radical Rudi Dutschke active during the cultural revolution of the '60s and '70s and before him the Italian Marxist Antonio Gramsci. Instead of overthrowing Western societies and establishing a socialist utopia by direct means using violence and force the strategy is to infiltrate and take control of the institutions underpinning society. (See also critical theory and the Frankfurt School.) The expression the is also associated with the communist dictator Chairman Mao who was responsible for the murder, torture, starvation and death of millions of Chinese during his reign of terror.

304. **Theory.** Associated with the cultural-left and the dominance of critical theory the term "theory" refers to a rainbow alliance of theories, including Marxism, neo-

Marxism, feminist, gender, queer and post-colonial theories. While often in disagreement all see Western civilisation as oppressive and are directed at overthrowing capitalism and those institutions seen as misogynist, heteronormative, racist, elitist and binary.

305. **The Other.** Drawing on critical theory and aspects of *Orientalism* the'other'refers to the way more dominant and powerful groups in society or nation states justify their crimes by labelling those being exploited and oppressed as the 'other' Categorising LGBTIQ+ people, women and people of colour as outside what is considered acceptable and normal makes it easier to justify their exclusion and mistreatment.

306. **Thicc.** Originating as a term used by African-Americans to describe women with voluptuous Rubens like figures and defined by the *Urban Dictionary* as a person who has "fat in the right places, creating sexy curves". After using the term "Thicc" to describe a curvaceous sea otter a Californian aquarium was criticised for equating African-Americans with animals and for cultural appropriation.

307. **Toxic Masculinity.** Refers to masculine characteristics and qualities that second and third wave feminists argue are sexist, violent and misogynist. Toxic masculinity leads to sexual exploitation and commodification of women, domestic violence and men being insensitive and closed

emotionally. Camille Paglia argues the expression is unfair as it demonstrates a "peevish, grudging rancour against men" where "men's faults, failings, and foibles have been seized on and magnified into gruesome bills of indictment".

308. **Toxic positivity.** Described as employers pressuring employees to be positive, confident and on top of things even though they are anxious and depressed from overwork and having to work in a negative environment.

309. **Tradwife.** Wendy Squires (*The Age*, 22 February 2020), even though she argues she would never want to be a "subservient tradwife", suggests such women have the right to free choice. She argues it is unfair for feminists to criticise women who are happy to be wives and mothers instead of pursuing a professional career. Squires describes a tradwife as a woman who "wants to bake up a storm, iron his shirts, believe her place is in the home and actively parent as a priority".

310. **Trans-erasure.** Dr Yves Rees, an academic at Melbourne's La Trobe University, describes trans-erasure as cis-people dominating the debate about transgenderism to the exclusion of trans people. After listing those questioning transgenderism, including J.K. Rowling and *Guardian* columnist Suzanne Moore, Rees writes "You know what's missing? Actual trans people. It's almost as if the trans issue only becomes newsworthy when powerful cisgender people

choose to comment" (*The Age*, 7 December 2010).

311. **Trans-exclusionary/trans-sceptical.** A thought crime committed by those daring to question whether individuals can change their birth sex and assume the identity of their biological opposite. (See also TERF standing for trans-exclusionary, radical feminist.)

312. **Transphobia.** The material associated with the Safe Schools gender and sexuality program defines transphobia as the "fear and hatred of gender diverse or transgender people, their desires and behaviours, that often leads to discrimination or abuse". Stopping boys who self-identify as girls from using female toilets and change rooms in schools is an example of transphobia as are parents counselling their children against undergoing gender transition.

Stopping transwomen from taking part in female sports is also an example of transphobia. A Canadian cyclist who was born as a man and who transitioned, Rachel McKinnon, argues anyone who complains ciswomen in sport are disadvantaged is politically incorrect. McKinnon argues it's a human rights issue and not a matter of being physically advantaged "We shouldn't be worried about transpeople taking over the Olympics. We should be worried about their fairness and human rights instead".

Juliet Macur, in an article published in *The New York Times*, cites an opposing view given by Dr Eric Vilain who argues “Now I’m really worried about the future of women in sports because if we push this argument, anyone declaring a female gender can compete as a woman. We’re moving toward one big competition, and the very predictable result of that competition is that there will be no women winners.” The champion tennis player Martina Navratilova is also concerned arguing “It is surely unfair on women who have to compete against people, biologically, who are still men”. Even though a strong supporter of the LGBTIQ+ community Navratilova has been criticised for her comments by Rachael McKinnon, a world champion transgender cyclist, arguing on the LGBT website Out that Navratilova’s comments are “disturbing, upsetting, and deeply transphobic”.

313. **Transgender.** The ‘Gender Questioning’ booklet published by Gay and Lesbian Health Victoria & Rainbow Network Victoria describes transgender as referring to “a large range of people whose common experience is that their inner sense of gender is different to the sex they were assigned at birth”. Gender is defined as fluid and limitless and the booklet states “There is no right or wrong in this, it’s about figuring out what feels right for you”.

314. **Transgenderism.** The media organisation GLAAD warns against using the description transgenderism as it “is not a term commonly used by transgender people. This is a term used by anti-transgender activists to dehumanize transgender people and reduce who they are to ‘a condition’”.

315. **Transpeople.** The 'Gender Questioning' booklet suggests individuals have the right to identify as "being male, female, something other or in between" and that as a result they can be either "lesbian, gay, bisexual, queer, straight or something else". Words used to describe transpeople include: "Transwomen, Transman, Transguy, Trannyboy, boi, Trannygirl, Trans masculine, Trans feminine, Tranz, bi-gendered, third sex, poly gendered, transbutch, transfag, trannydyke, androgyne".

316. **Trigger warnings.** The British academic Frank Furedi describes how trigger warnings originated in universities and campuses in North America to protect snowflake students who might be offended by material encountered during their studies. Examples include poems, plays and novels that are "assigned a health warning to indicate that they contain scenes of domestic violence, sexism, racism or a variety of other pathologies". Examples include the Greek tragedy *Media* that involves domestic violence and filicide, Marvell's poem *To His Coy Mistress* that commodifies women and *Hamlet* where Ophelia commits suicide.

317. **Trolling/trolled.** Evita March on *The Conversation* website defines online trolling as "deceptive and disruptive online behaviour which typically involves posting inflammatory and malicious comments to deliberately provoke and upset people". An example of trolling involves the often racist and

offensive online remarks directed at Meghan Markle causing her friend George Clooney to go public saying "she has been pursued and vilified and chased in the same way that Diana was and it's history repeating itself".

318. **Trope.** *The Cambridge Dictionary* defines trope as "something such as an idea, phrase, or image that is often used in a particular artist's work, in a particular type of art". In Hollywood movies and TV shows, to overcome heteronormativity and to promote woke gender theory, it's no obligatory to have at least one scene involving non-binary actors involved in an intimate relationship.

319. **Trump derangement syndrome.** Fareed Zakaria is quoted in the Australian edition of *The Spectator* as describing TDS as a "hatred of President Trump so intense that it impairs people's judgement and has led to well-respected columnists describing him as a 'fascist', a 'white supremacist' and a 'Nazi'".

320. **Twitterati.** The *Urban Dictionary* describes the twitterati as "The Tweet elite, whose feeds attract thousands of followers and whose 140-character spews capture the attention of the rapt who doggedly monitor them".

321. **Two-spirit.** A native American expression describing a person who identifies as being male and female.

322. **Unconscious bias.** It is not only unacceptable to display or advocate politically incorrect language and behaviour – equally as bad is being guilty of unconscious bias. The Australian Public Service Commission warns against what is described as "unintended discrimination"; a situation where even though you never intended to cause offence you are guilty and need to be re-educated. The Commission's website includes research by the Australian National University that lists 150 examples of unconscious bias, including: stereotyping marginalised individuals and groups, defending the status quo, group think and confirmation bias.

323. **Vegan.** The *Urban Dictionary* describes a vegan as somebody "who slaughters and kills fruits and vegetables". Shareena Hamzah from the UK's Swansea University believes such is the popularity of veganism and vegetarianism that meat eating will soon be under threat; especially as it is so unhealthy and because it contributes to global warming. As a result, Hamzah argues the language and expressions we use when referring to animals will change and she quotes a number of examples from the People for the Ethical Treatment of Animals. (See also non-animalistic language.)

324. **Vegetative state.** Once used to describe people who are disabled to such a degree that they do not appear conscious and are unable to communicate, as in "Vegetative woman gives birth in care". Vegans consider the description offensive as it demeans vegetables and ignores the fact they are 'alive'

and able to respond to their environment. Alternatives include "comatose" or "an individual of alternative, non-binary perception, communication and movement".

325. **Vertically challenged.** A non-judgemental term used to describe short people. For example "Snow White enjoyed the friendship and company of seven vertically challenged, no-gendered individuals". (See also short shaming.)

326. **Victim revisionism.** Involves the process whereby those self-identifying as victims rewrite the past to ensure their victim status is affirmed.

327. **Virtuous masculinity.** The American Pastor Jeff Sanders and drawing on the Bible describes a virtuous man as one who is a provider, a leader and someone who can earn respect and show compassion, integrity and faith.

328. **Virtue signalling.** The *Urban Dictionary* describes this as taking "a conspicuous but essentially useless action ostensibly to support a good cause but actually to show off how much more moral you are than everyone else". Businesses and corporations virtue signal by championing causes related to the environment, Indigenous affairs and gender equality to disguise the fact their primary aim is to make a profit. An example involves the head of BHP, Andrew Mackenzie, arguing that fossil fuels represent an "existential risk" to

the planet while his company continues to make millions in profit each year involving coal and petroleum.

329. **Western Civilisation.** Despite being responsible for developing a political and legal system that ensures freedom and liberty and guarantees human rights; initiating the industrial and digital revolutions; providing increased standards of living and scientific and medical revolutions, Western civilisation has no right to be considered more beneficial or preferable compared to any other civilisation. To do so is to be guilty of white supremacism and Western essentialism.

Ignored, as argued by Steven Pinker in *Enlightenment Now: The Case For Reason, Science, Humanism And Progress,* is that not all cultures are equal and that Western civilisation, for all its flaws, deserves special recognition. Pinker argues that beginning with the Enlightenment and continuing with industrial, scientific and technological advances, Western civilisation is responsible for an unprecedented period of prosperity and growth that has improved the health and living standards of billions across the globe.

330. **WEIRD.** Stands for the majority of university leaders, including chancellors and vice-chancellors, who are always Western, Educated, Industrialised, Rich and Democratic. According to Melbourne University academics Siew Fang Law and Gwilym Croucher in a piece published on

The Conversation website "In 2018 of the 699 governing council roles across Australia's 41 universities, 94% of the incumbents had Caucasian and British backgrounds. The top tiers of senior executives were 94% Caucasian and British in background, as were 96% of vice-chancellors".

331. **Wellness whitewash.** The Melbourne woke activist Rachel Akhidenor argues the meditation and wellness movement is dominated by "one type of person – white, female, thin and privileged" (*The Age*, 24 January 2021). People of colour are excluded and Akhidenor argues it's time to change wellness "from being a very elitist, white thing to being accessible by everyone".

332. **Whinja ninjas.** The Australian Catholic University's Anthony Dillon uses the expression to describe those Woke Activists and members of the Aboriginal victim brigade who vilified and attacked the cartoonist Bill Leak for his depiction of an Aboriginal father for not knowing his son's name. In his chapter in *Cancel Culture and the Left's Long March* Dillion writes "While the 'woke', the Aboriginal victim brigade, the offendarati (a term coined by Bill), and the whinja ninjas went nuts about the cartoon on social media, Australia's highest-ranking Aboriginal police officer, my father, Col Dillon, praised Bill for it. In a long and distinguished career my father has seen it all and instantly recognised the message Bill was communicating".

333. **Whiteness.** Dr Omid Tofighian from the University of Sydney condemns the traditional curriculum for enforcing "whiteness"; defined as a curriculum that is Eurocentric, oppressive and complicit in denying the "identity and cultural background of marginalised groups". According to Tofighian subjects like history, literature, art and music must be radically overhauled as they are guilty of "racism, sexism, classism, historical injustice and prejudice based on religion". (*The Conversation* website, 5 October 2015). The University of London's Collective argues that "whiteness" promotes power and thought which is "racialized as white" and "heteropatriarchally/cisgenderly male".

Paul T Le and Cheryl E Matais describe "whiteness" as a "hegemonic racial dominance that has become so natural it is almost invisible". They suggest science education is not immune from the evils of "whiteness" by arguing their research "identifies how whiteness operates in science education such that it falls short of its goal for cultural diversity". The South Australian curriculum also argues as science is a socio/cultural construct with no right to be considered preeminent that "Western science is the most dominant form of science but it is only one form among the sciences of the world". (See also Aboriginal and Torres Strait Islander Science.)

334. **White feminism.** Zofiya Acosta defines this as "feminism that refuses to be intersectional and only caters to empower women with privilege. It is not a blanket term for feminists

who happen to be white. Instead, it's a way to call out people who promote feminism but stay mum on issues that affect women who have less privilege". Campaigning to get more women onto corporate boards does nothing to alleviate the violence suffered by Indigenous women living in remote Aboriginal communities.

335. **White saviour complex.** Faima Bakar on the Metro website describes this as when "a white person who acts to help non-white people, but in a context which can be perceived as self-serving. When white celebrities pose with an African child or praise unfortunate and vulnerable people for being brave and stoic, there is an element of privilege that adds to the controversial trope".

336. **White saviour industrial complex.** The twitter Teju Cole argues "the fastest growth industry in the US is the White Saviour Industrial Complex". Instead of genuinely believing is alleviating racism, injustice and poverty wealthy, elitist Americans are more concerned with validating their own sense of self-worth and self-esteem.

337. **White-splaining.** Described as white supremacists ignoring and silencing the voices of people of colour.

338. **White supremacism**. A New South Wales school curriculum official once cited *The Three Little Pigs* as an example of white supremacism. Instead of being an

innocent children's story it "contains elements of a world view which the British authorities, if not all the convicts, brought to Australia in 1788. The story assumes a society with private property and individualised labour. It applauds discipline and hard work and the solid stone or brick houses of Europe, it places non-material cultural pursuits second to material, and its primary motivation comes from fear of nature, or wilderness, in the form of a wolf. It could not be an Aboriginal folk tale or Dreaming story".

339. **White Privilege.** Those, through no fault of their own, who are of European and Anglo/Celtic descent are guilty of "whiteness" as they are inherently privileged and guilty of oppressing and disadvantaging victim groups. As such, they must be re-educated to ensure they are aware of their prejudices and atone for their sins – either conscious or unconscious. A guideline for the re-education of nurses and midwives guilty of "whiteness" refers to adopting an approach that involves "a decolonising model of practice based on dialogue, communication, power sharing and negotiation, and the acknowledgment of white privilege". A South Australian government department also asks employees to acknowledge white privilege when undertaking Indigenous sensitivity training on the basis that "We seek to better recognise the influence colonisation and white privilege has (sic) on the department's internal and external interactions with Aboriginal people, their nations and communities, and guide opportunities for reconciliation into the future".

340. **White tears.** As a result of the Collingwood Football Club being accused of systemic racism the president Eddie McGuire was pressured to resign. The Australian Greens Party Senator Lydia Thorpe used the expression "white tears" when describing McGuire's emotional resignation speech. The implication being such tears have no value or worth as McGuire is a white privileged male who does not deserve any pity.

341. **Whitewashing.** Described as employing white actors and actresses to play the part of a non-white character, thus, further marginalising and oppressing people of colour. Ruby Hamad on Australia's SBS website argues the lack of racial diversity in the media is a sign of prejudice. He writes "With Australia's default setting firmly set to 'white,' it is not surprising that in a social climate that still prioritises white voices, bigotry is on the rise".

342. **Woke.** Refers to being able define oneself and to see others and the wider world through a politically correct prism. The *Urban Dictionary* defines this as "A reference to how people should be aware in current affairs". As in "While you worried whether you could order a decaf, freetrade, almond milk latte, China was building over 100 coal fired power stations, stay WOKE".

343. **Woke capitalism.** Refers to businesses and corporations championing woke causes, individuals and events to

demonstrate they are committed to equity, justice and overcoming threats like global warming. Helen Lewis in *The Atlantic* questions the sincerity of woke capitalism when suggesting "Progressive values are now a powerful branding tool" and "Those with power inside institutions love splashy progressive gestures—solemn, monochrome social-media posts deploring racism; appointing their first woman to the board; firing low-level employees who attract online fury—because they help preserve their power". (See also virtue signalling.)

344. **Wokeington principle.** As detailed by *The Australian* newspaper's The Mocker, the wokeington principle has recently replaced one of the foundation stones of British common law - the presumption of innocence and the conviction no-one can be declared guilty until they have been convicted by the court according to the law. The mocker writes "Henceforth the rule in Woolmington will be replaced by the Wokeington Principle. In certain cases, people will still enjoy the presumption of innocence and the entitlement to legal representation, but only at the say so of the virtuous.

345. **Wokery.** The *Urban Dictionary* defines this as "Today's hottest religion. Joining it allows simple-minded people to pride themselves on believing they are more enlightened than, more compassionate than, and morally superior to, most of their fellow (unwoke) human beings".

346. **Wokescold.** Involves being scolded and criticised for not being woke in relation to PC issues and debates. The American academic Rod Dreher recounts being attacked by a student after he praised the iconic photo of the sailor kissing the nurse in Times Square at the end of World War II. The student argued it was an example of sexual assault and that the sailor "should have gone to jail".

347. **Wokeism.** Michael Karson on the *Psychology Today* website defines wokeism as "a system of thought and behavior characterized by intolerance, policing the speech of others, and proving one's own superiority by denouncing others".

348. **Women shaming**. See slut shaming.

349. **Worry porn**: Chris Mitchell in *The Australian* (24 January 2022), drawing on the American journalist Holman W. Jenkins, uses the expression "worry porn" to describe the media reporting events and issues in a sensational and exaggerated way. Usually employed by woke journalists with issues like climate change and the evil nature of President Trump and his supporters, worry porn forsakes any semblance of impartiality and balance to win approval.

350. **Wrongthink.** In her letter of resignation as an editor and columnist for *The New York Times* Bari Weiss complains she was often criticised for wrongthink. She argues the paper is

so consumed with pushing a progressive liberal agenda and conforming to politically correct ideology that it no longer presents news and opinion is a balanced, impartial way. Wrongthink is to commit the crime of thinking independently and not following the dictates of politically correct group think. (See also George Orwell's concept of Thoughtcrime.)

351. **Yellow facing.** Similar to black facing this is an example of cultural appropriation where a white person assumes the identity of an Asian. The Melbourne comedian Cate Hanley Corley was forced to withdraw her comic act involving Aisha the Aussie Geisha from the Fringe Festival after an open letter signed by approximately 70 people criticised her. The letter argued Corley's act "borders on yellow face" as it "revolves around the belittling and insulting depiction of Asian peoples for cheap humour". Another example involves Vietnamese-Australian lawyer Cat-Thao Nguyen who after seeing a production of the opera *Turandot* in Sydney argued it was deeply offensive and an example of cultural appropriation. Apparently, having white actors and singers with painted faces and wearing traditional Chinese peasant costumes perpetuated racism.

352. **Ze and zie.** A neutral, non-gendered pronoun used instead of "he" or "she", "him" or "her". As in "The non-binary, gender free person told me zie will be here tomorrow".

THE BRAVE NEW WORLD OF WOKE

In the context of Western societies, "the long march through the institutions" signified – in the words of Herbert Marcuse – "working against the established institutions while working in them". It was primarily by this means – by insinuation and infiltration rather than concentration – that the countercultural dreams of radicals like Marcuse have triumphed.

Roger Kimball, *The Long March*

Those defending political correctness (now rebadged as being woke) argue it is a form of politeness and civility and it is beneficial as it pressures people to treat others with fairness and respect. There is an element of truth in such an argument as it is wrong to unfairly vilify and denigrate others because of who they are, their beliefs or their way of life. There's no place for racism, misogyny, homophobia, sexism or classism in a fair and open society. What the cultural-left ignores, judged by the *Human Freedom Index 2020* published by the Cato and Fraser institutes and based on a 2017–2018 index, is that Western nations overwhelmingly dominate the top 20 positions. Based on characteristics such as the rule of law, personal security and freedom of movement, speech, religion and assembly it's obvious the countries considered the freest include New Zealand, Switzerland, Denmark, Sweden, Finland, Australia, Canada, the United Kingdom and the United States. (Note: while Hong Kong was previously ranked number 3, since China's authoritarian and undemocratic intervention it is no longer seen as a bastion of freedom.)

As previously mentioned, while PC pretends to be about overcoming disadvantage and promoting equity and freedom the reality is it is underpinned by radical, cultural-left ideology that can be traced back to neo-Marxism and the emergence of critical theory. Central to the left's long march is the decision to take control of institutions including schools and universities, church, family, media, political organisations and movements and intermediary organisations such as trade unions and professional associations.

It is no accident that Australia's Roz Ward justifies the gender fluidity Safe Schools program in terms of Marxist ideology or that much of the sociology of education portrays schools and education as servants of capitalism – describing them as an essential part of the ideological state apparatus used to reinforce the power of the elites and to further disadvantage those, such as the working class, women, LGBTIQ+ people and people of colour, already oppressed. American commentators, including the Heritage Foundation's Mike Gonzalez, also argue communism underpins the radical Black Lives Matter movement that became a world-wide phenomenon after the death of George Floyd at the hands of a Minneapolis policeman in May 2020.

Since Friedrich Engels and Karl Marx published *The Communist Manifesto* in 1848 and wrote "workers of the world unite!" communism has been one of the most powerful and influential ideologies shaping world history. Whether the Russian revolution and the rise of the USSR as a world power or the impact of communism in China, South-East Asia and South America communism has impacted on the lives of millions and millions of people.

Central to communism is the ideal "from each according to their ability, to each according to their needs" and the belief capitalist societies, the right to own private property and to make a profit are inherently unjust and oppressive. If the revolution is to succeed, the workers must overthrow the status quo and take control of the state apparatus and the modes and means of production. As proven by what happened under Lenin and Stalin in the USSR and Mao in China, if violence and terror are what is required to achieve the workers' paradise then the end will always justify the means. When discussing the nihilistic and evil nature of communism Del Noce writes in *The Ascendence of Eroticism*:

> *There is no separation between ends and means since these latter are organically subordinated to whatever goal has been discerned from the evolution of history. Hence, ever kind of violence, every ruse, every illegal action, every dissimulation, and every deception become licit if they are deemed to be necessary to reach the goal. This is the classical thesis of Marx-Leninism, which says politics absorbs morality within itself, and it would seem there could not be a more radical violation of the traditional moral code.*

In this Machiavellian world of political and social action there is no right or wrong based on what is ethical or morally good, there is simply the desire to gain power for power's sake. Hence the need to destroy Christianity and to replace religious faith with worshiping the glorious leader destined to bring about a utopia on this earth, replacing the city of God with the city man. As argued by Mao Zedong "Political power grows out of the barrel of a gun". In China, as a result, during Mao's reign of terror over 50 million Chinese died because of starvation, torture and execution. And as so clearly illustrated in George Orwell's *Animal Farm* while communism and its comrade in arms socialism begin with the promise of equality and freedom for all they quickly descend into violence and oppression where those in charge impose a totalitarian regime. A regime in many ways worse than what the revolution replaced.

Under Stalin millions also died, starved and were imprisoned and citizens faced a bleak and barren life compared to those in the West where capitalism, Christianity and liberalism ensured prosperity and a standard of living far beyond what communism could ever provide. In Cambodia under Pol Pot's reign of terror approximately two million died, the country was bankrupted and those who survived lived in daily terror. Cuba and Venezuela provide other examples of how oppressive and inhumane communism is as the individual liberties and rights we, in the West, take for granted as our birthright are denied.

As noted in the introduction to this dictionary, the origins of political correctness and wokeism can be traced to a number of intellectuals and academics associated with the Frankfurt School established in Germany during the 1920s. In addition to becoming dissatisfied with communism the intellectuals involved also realised such was the relative prosperity and freedom experienced by those living in the West there was little, if any, chance of the disaffected storming the barricades and using violence to take control.

The focus of the revolution shifted from the economy to what has become known as the culture wars. Michael Gove in *Celsius* describes this as a time when in order to overthrow the status quo and radically change society the focus had to be "less and less on workers' struggles and instead (become) engaged in wider battles". Gove especially notes the rise of identity politics because of what is described as the long march through the institutions. Del Noce makes a similar point when arguing "It is clear that what today is called the left fights less and less in terms of class warfare, and more and more in terms of 'warfare against repression'". Whether repression caused by society being Eurocentric, homophobic, sexist, heteronormative or misogynist the fight to overthrow capitalist society is now focused on winning the culture wars.

One of the most significant theories associated with the Frankfurt School is critical theory – defined by the *Stanford Encyclopedia of Philosophy* as a liberating and emancipatory philosophy directed at "decreasing domination and increasing freedom in all its forms". Whether freeing those oppressed by capitalism, racism, sexism or a heteronormative, binary sense of gender and sexuality the purpose of critical theory is to overthrow the status quo and initiate a new period of equality and freedom for all.

The Encyclopedia goes on to suggest in order to qualify as critical theory what is being advocated "must explain what is wrong with current social reality, identify the actors to change it, and provide both clear norms for criticism and achievable practical goals for social transformation". As with communism, the emphasis is very much on social transformation on the basis that existing capitalist societies are rife with injustice and inequality.

It is impossible to underestimate the impact of critical theory on universities and schools in subjects like sociology, history, literature, geography, science, mathematics and politics. As previously mentioned, literary texts are now critiqued in terms of power relationships associated with gender, ethnicity and class and history no longer deals with the grand narrative associated with the rise and evolution of Western civilisation. If Western civilisation is mentioned, it is usually through a black armband perspective. Such is the pervasive nature of critical theory and its recent offspring post-colonial theory, mathematics and science have also become victims of cultural-left ideology. The Australian national curriculum includes the statement Aborigines, even though a primitive culture compared to the West, "are adept at pattern and algebraic thinking" and the curriculum is "structured around identified themes in Aboriginal and Torres Strait Islander Peoples' mathematical thinking, understandings and processes". So much for Pythagoras and Euclidean geometry.

Gove also makes the point the cultural revolution of the mid to late 1960s saw a rebirth of critical theory as a significant and powerful force for radical change. Illustrated by the 1968 student riots in Paris, Woodstock and the hippy, counter-culture movement, the emergence of radical feminism, gender and LGBTIQ+ theories this was a time, as Wordsworth observed about the French Revolution of 1789, "bliss was it in that dawn to be alive, but to be young was very heaven". While there is no doubt aspects of Western culture and the institutions and way of life associated with it were, and still are, in need of correction and improvement what occurred represents a far more radical and destructive attack.

As noted by the Australian art critic Giles Auty in *Culture At Crisis Point* the '60s cultural revolution represented a significant and far reaching social, intellectual and cultural change that critiqued and undermined the very foundations of Western societies.

> *What "the long march" has attempted is not just the overthrow of Western culture in a narrow sense but a rewriting of the moral and civil codes which underwrite the entire God-inspired history of Western civilisation.*

The American author Roger Kimball is his book *The Long March* also suggests that the cultural revolution of the late '60s signified a dramatic and far-reaching change in the way the cultural-left sought to radically remake society in its image. Kimball writes in relation to America, "In a democratic society such as ours, where free elections are guaranteed, political revolution is almost unthinkable in practical terms. Consequently, utopian attempts to transform society have been channelled into cultural and moral life".

Whether the anti-war movement and race riots, student activism on campus, the sexual revolution brought about by the birth control pill or the Dionysian culture of immediate physical gratification, the end result was long held and accepted beliefs and institutions were attacked and undermined. The concept of Western culture being beneficial or preferable was especially targeted by the cultural-left's long march through the institutions. As noted by Arthur

M. Schlesinger, Jr in *The Disuniting of America* this was a time when:

> *The Western tradition, in this view, is inherently racist, sexist, "classist", hegemonic; irredeemably repressive, irredeemably oppressive. The spread of Western culture is due not to any innate quality but simply to the spread of Western power.*

Schlesinger also makes the point for all its faults and shortcomings compared to other cultures Western civilisation contains within itself the ability to identify and critique its flaws and injustices and to move towards greater freedom, equality and justice for all.

> *There remains a crucial difference between the Western tradition and the others. The crimes committed by the West have produced their own antidotes. They have produced great movements to end slavery, to raise the status of women, to abolish torture, to combat racism, to defend freedom of inquiry and expression, to advance personal liberty and human rights.*

While woke activists argue it's wrong to criticise or find fault in indigenous cultures the reality is many were, and still are, characterised by practices such as child brides, slavery and the exploitation and subjugation of women. And there are still countries like Saudi Arabia, Brunei and the United Arab Emirates that embrace a fundamentalist view of Islam were practices like female circumcision, the victimisation of LGBTIQ+ people and treating women as inferior are prevalent and considered acceptable.

WOKE IDEOLOGY AND GROUP THINK – AUSTRALIA AS A CASE STUDY

In the long march through the institutions, reforms must be sought that satisfy the immediate needs of students, teachers, and parents. Pie-in-the-sky politics must be rejected in favour of a program of revolutionary reforms built around such issues as democracy, free classrooms, open enrollment, adequate financial aid for needy students, and development of a critical antidiscriminatory and socialist content of education.

Bowles and Gintis, *Schooling in Capitalist America*

The above quotation exemplifies how the cultural-left defines the purpose of education; one where the curriculum and how schools are managed and organised is directed at overthrowing the status quo and heralding a socialist inspired utopia. Opposing this ideological approach is a liberal view of education. An education that is concerned with the formation of virtues and character and that can be traced back to the ancient Roman and Greek sophists and philosophers.

A liberal view of education is based on the conviction knowledge is inherently worthwhile and to be educated is to be familiar with those disciplines and areas of learning that constitute a well-balanced, comprehensive and rigorous educational experience. While evolving and growing over the years (the curriculum is no longer restricted to Latin, Greek, Grammar, Rhetoric and Logic) schools generally introduce students to a defined body of knowledge, understanding and skills and a particular disposition and way of seeking understanding and truth. Professor Brian Crittenden in *Cultural Pluralism and Common Curriculum* defines this liberal view of education as:

> *... in effect, a systematic and sustained introduction to those public forms of meaning in which the standards of human excellence in the intellectual, moral and aesthetic domains are expressed and critically investigated.*

The English poet and inspector of schools Matthew Arnold's phrase "the best that has been thought and said" is often referred to when suggesting what constitutes a worthwhile and beneficial education. And it should be noted critics generally ignore the second half of what Arnold argues when he states it is vital to turn "fresh and free thought upon our stock habits and notions". Cultural conservatism is as much about change and evolution as it is about acknowledging and holding on to what has gone before. As noted by T.S. Eliot, equally as important as acknowledging and valuing the past is the realisation that cultures and societies do evolve. Eliot writes in *The Aims of Education*, the purpose of education is:

> *... to maintain the continuity of our culture – and neither continuity, nor a respect for the past, implies standing still. More than ever, we look to education today to preserve*

us from the error of pure contemporaneity. We look to institutions of education to maintain a knowledge and understanding of the past.

Significant is that the Italian communist Antonio Gramsci argues if the oppressed are to be liberated from capitalism they must be educated. In *Selections from the Prison Notebooks* Gramsci speaks favourably about learning Latin and Greek and the benefits of an education centred on "the interior development of personality, the formation of character by means of the absorption and assimilation of the whole cultural past of modern European civilisation".

In their seminal book *Schooling in Capitalist America* (published in 1976) two American academics, Samuel Bowles and Herbert Gintis, present one of the most direct attacks on a liberal view of education. Instead of schools and what is taught being inherently worthwhile or beneficial they argue "inequities in education are part of the capitalist system and are likely to persist as long as capitalism survives". Building on a Marxist critique of society the argument is schools are a critical part of the ideological state apparatus that reproduces inequality and indoctrinates future citizens to accept their subservient role.

While individuals might believe that they are free and in control of their destiny and that education is a worthwhile pursuit they only do so because they have been conditioned and are victims of false consciousness. Meritocracy, competition and focusing on academic studies are all tools employed by capitalist society to strengthen and reproduce itself.

Drawing on Marxist and cultural-left inspired intellectuals including

Pierre Bourdieu, Michael W. Apple. M F. D. Young, Louise Althusser and in Australia Bob Connell and Bill Hannan this radical attack on the schools has had a profound effect. Joan Kirner, the one-time Victorian Minister for Education and Premier, champions this Marxist view of education in a speech given at a conference organised by the Victorian Fabian Society in 1983. Kirner argues:

> *If we are egalitarian in our intention, we have to reshape education so that is part of the socialist struggle for equality, participation and social change, rather than an instrument for the capitalist system.*

As such, equality of opportunity must be replaced by equality of outcomes; a situation where positive discrimination involving quotas is needed to ensure so-called victim groups and the disadvantaged no longer suffer because of an elitist and oppressive education system.

In Australia, one of the most strident and effective advocates of a cultural-left view of the purpose of education and the relationship between schools and society is the Australian Education Union (AEU) and one of its predecessors, the Australian Teachers' Federation (ATF). Since the mid-to-late-1960s both organisations have argued against the academic curriculum, competitive examinations, standardised literacy and numeracy testing and government funding for non-government schools. The ATF's 1985 curriculum policy describes Australian society as one characterised by:

- *The pronounced inequality in the distribution of social, economic, cultural and political resources and power between social groups, which restricts the life development of many.*

- *The role of the economy, the sexual division of labour, the dominant culture and the education system in reproducing inequality.*

It should not surprise the Australian Education Union, in addition to arguing that schools must be radically overhauled, advocates a politically correct ideology in areas such as the environment, Indigenous affairs, multiculturalism, refugees, gender and sexuality, funding non-government schools and Australia's involvement in the Iraqi war after the 9/11 attacks in America.

The AEU's 2003 'Policy on gay, lesbian, bisexual and transgender people' argues Australian society and its institutions, including schools and churches, promote homophobia and heterosexism and schools have a major role to play in advancing the rights of GLBT people. The policy also states it is wrong to believe there is anything natural or normal about heterosexual sex and relationships and that "All curriculum should be written in non-heterosexist language" and "homosexuality and bisexuality need to be normalised".

The union, to justify its policy in related material, argues 9-11% of the population identify as exclusively same sex attracted and another 10% of the population identify as bisexual. The paper concludes "Thus at any one stage 20% of the population would not identify with a heterosexual lifestyle". Ignored, as previously mentioned, is that according to a national survey carried out by

La Trobe University academics approximately 98% of Australians surveyed identify as either women or men. In a second national survey published in the *Australian and New Zealand Journal of Public Health* (Vol 27, No 2) involving 10,173 men and 9,134 women the results also disprove the exaggerated claims made by those seeking to normalise LGBTIQ+ lifestyles. In this second survey 97.4% of men and 97.7% of women identify as heterosexual.

The teacher union's opposition to Prime Minister John Howard's decision to support America in the Iraqi invasion after 9/11 also displays a cultural-left perspective. In a media release dated 17 January 2003 the union argues that there is "absolutely no justification" for the invasion and that the Howard Government is guilty of promoting "militarism and xenophobia". In a second media release, dated 20 March, the Australian Education Union argues against the "illegal invasion of Iraq" and teachers are urged to "support students who take anti-war stance" and to "encourage participation in peaceful protests with the support and involvement of other family members".

More recently the AEU has been a consistent and vocal supporter of primary and secondary students taking time off school to attend a series of national climate-day strikes generally held during the school week on a Friday. The AEU President Correna Haythorpe in a media release dated 8 March 2019 states "The AEU supports the democratic right of students to take direct action, giving voice to their real concerns about the impacts of climate change, and protesting the inaction by the federal government". In the educational jargon much loved by PC educators Haythorpe goes on to say, "Our students must be equipped with the right skills to become innovators and agents of change in a rapidly changing world" and "Climate change is a reality and the only acceptable debate is about how we deal with the consequences and ensure that our children and students are prepared for the future".

Since 2019 teacher unions have become even more strident in their support of student activism. Australia's peak education unions, including the Australian Education Union, the Independent Education Union and the National Tertiary Education Union, under the heading 'Education unions proudly support students strike for climate', the unions boast "Together we represent more than 200,000 members working in the education sector. As teachers and educators we bear witness to the will, determination and passion alive in our students in their fight for action on climate change on a daily basis".

Even though approximately 34% of Australian students attend non-government schools (20% Catholic and 14% independent) and the major political parties support parental choice and government funding the AEU also adopts a politically correct approach to choice and diversity in education. The union has a long history of opposing the existence of non-government schools evidenced by a 1985 policy document that describes such schools as "selective rather than comprehensive with many devoted to the social elite".

The union goes on to argue the "dual system of schooling is a pronounced cause of inequalities of educational outcomes" and that "the resource efforts of government should be wholly devoted to the public systems which are open to all". Ignored is the existence, especially in Sydney, of selective government schools that are not open to all students and the fact not all parents are able to afford the cost of expensive real estate in the enrolment zones of many academically successful government schools.

More recently, in its response to the 2011 Gonski review of school funding and in subsequent debates about what constitutes a fair and equitable funding system, the AEU continues its opposition to governments financially supporting Catholic and independent schools:

> *Although substantial government funding to private schools has become entrenched in Australia in recent decades, we believe there is no pre-existing, pre-determined entitlement to public funding, i.e. there is no a priori justification for public funding to private schools.*

How English is defined and taught as a subject provides further evidence of how successful the cultural-left has been in enforcing its ideology on schools. With reading and how students are expected to respond to literature, drawing originally on the works of the South American Marxist Paulo Freire, the focus is very much on what is described a critical literacy.

Freire condemns the more traditional approach to teaching English as "massification" – a situation where instead of thinking critically and independently students are forced to acquiesce to the process and be submissive. Practices like rote learning, teachers as experts and failing to address real-life issues are also criticised as promoting a "banking concept" where learners, supposedly, are passive and treated as empty vessels waiting to be filled with knowledge.

Critical literacy, on the other hand and much like critical theory, argues learning a language and education more broadly must be emancipatory and liberating. Drawing on Marxist theory Freire argues the true purpose of education is to allow students "to perceive themselves in dialectical relationship with their social reality... to assume an increasingly critical attitude toward the world and so to transform it". Within Australia academics in charge of teacher education and professional bodies like the Australian Association for the Teaching of English and the Australian Curriculum Studies Association are staunch supporters of Freire's work and the concept of critical literacy. Two influential academics Walton and Luke, after noting the importance of a Critical Literacy conference held at Griffith University in 1992, suggest:

> *One of the recurring themes which emerged from the discussions and plenaries was the need to critique and re-work Freirian approaches to critical literacy, particularly in the light of feminist, poststructuralist and socially-based linguistics.*

An editorial written for a 2004 edition of *English in Australia*, bemoaning the re-election of the conservative Howard Commonwealth Government, also illustrates how pervasive this Marxist inspired approach to English is. The author, Wayne Sawyer, argues teachers had failed to adequately teach critical literacy and they must redouble their efforts as Howard being re-elected proved students were easily duped and not able to think clearly. Sawyer argues:

My main concern is with what the election tells us about our profession. English for the last ten years – not least on the pages of this journal – has trumpeted the cause of critical literacy ... What does it mean for us and our ability to create a questioning, critical generation that those who brought us balaclava'd security guards, Alsations and Patrick's Stevedoring could declare themselves the representatives of the workers and be supported by the electorate?

Critical literacy and associated feminist, gender, sexuality and post-colonial theories have also had, and continue to have, a significant impact on how literature as a school subject is now taught.

Literature before the cultural-left's campaign to take control was generally restricted to those novels, short stories, plays and poems that had something significant, profound and lasting to say about human nature, how people interact and relate to the wider world and how we perceive and cope with the myriad challenges and issues we have to deal with as we journey through life. As D. H. Lawrence suggests in an essay titled *Morality and the Novel,* the "business of art is to reveal the relation between man and his circumambient universe at the living moment". Good literature was also acknowledged and celebrated as the finest example of language use and where words, whether written or spoken, were crafted in such a way as to be evocative, memorable and exemplary.

Literature, especially Greek, Roman, Celtic and Norse myths, fables and legends, also deals with the predicaments, heroes, archetypes and feelings that underpin much of Western culture and that speak to our inner emotional and spiritual selves. Such archetypes and myths deal with love, betrayal, courage, sorrow, forgiveness and the need to find a more spiritual and transcendent sense of meaning in what is an often unforgiving, transient and challenging world. The stories and exploits of legendary heroines like Athena and Aphrodite and heroes like Odysseus, Beowulf and Thor still resonate today as evidenced by Hollywood movies like *Clash of the Titans, Wonder Women, Thor: Ragnarok* and the television series *Vikings*. The Bible is also centre place in dealing with what it means to be human, how best to find fulfilment and how best to lead the good life in a world characterised as a vale of tears.

Instead of focusing on the moral and aesthetic importance of literature, one where students learn to understand human nature and to empathise with others, the emphasis is now on deconstructing so-called texts in terms of power relationships and critical theory. In a paper delivered at a AATE National Conference, Maria Pallotta-Chiaarolli argues that the English classroom must be re-positioned as "a site of deconstructionist and interventionist strategies when challenging/resisting dominant discourses of marginalistaion and prejudice". Examples of prejudice include "homophobia, heterosexism and AIDS-discrimination" along with "racism, ethnocentrism, classism and sexism".

In a paper published by the American National Council of Teachers of English the argument is put that Shakespeare's *Romeo and Juliet* is in danger of reinforcing "heterosexist and misogynist messages" as it ignores the fact that "not all people are heterosexual or conform to traditional gender roles". As a result of critical literacy Conrad's *Heart of Darkness* is also criticised because of its treatment of slavery, *Moby Dick* as it centres on killing whales and Mark Twain's *Huckleberry Finn* because it includes the word "nigger".

The campaign to redefine literature even extends to children's books where *Little Black Samba* is politically incorrect as it disparages people of colour, *Thomas the Tank Engine* because it has a hierarchy of trains with the Fat Controller (the capitalist boss) in charge and *Cinderella* and *Snow White* because they reinforce a patriarchal view of the world where women are subservient to men and the happy ending is defined as a heterosexual marriage.

How history is taught in schools has also been dramatically redefined to make it politically correct. While no one is suggesting that schools and the curriculum should embrace an overly celebratory and positive approach, what the Australian Geoffrey Blainey describes as a "three cheers view of history", there is mounting evidence that what students are presented with unfairly undermines and critiques both Western civilisation and Australia's foundation as a penal colony and its evolution since 1788. As detailed by Stuart Macintyre in *The History Wars* more radical approaches emerged during the heady days of the Vietnam war moratoriums and the rise of the counter-culture movement. How Australian history was taught was especially affected:

> *In the 1960s and 1970s, critical approaches to Australian history questioned established interpretations of settlement and progress. Historians pursued voices frequently absent*

from the national narrative. Social historians of feminist, migrant and Aboriginal perspectives challenged the exclusiveness of traditional historical approaches.

This was a time when the grand narrative associated with the rise and development of Western civilisation increasingly came under attack as academics turned towards what Macintyre describes as "history from below" involving Marxist, feminist, gender and post-colonial theories. As a result, historians shifted the focus of history teaching to incorporate the treatment and perspectives of Indigenous Australians, gays and lesbians, recently arrived migrants and women.

How history is detailed in the Australian National Curriculum from the preparatory to year 10 illustrates how successful the cultural-left has been in redefining the subject. Like other subjects, students are told in the history curriculum that Australia is a multicultural, secular society characterised by diversity and difference and where various cultures, ethnic and race groups interact and live. Even though Australia owes much to Western civilisation, Judeo-Christianity and enlightenment values like rationality and reason the curriculum promotes a relativistic stance where all cultures and histories are treated equally and deserving of recognition and respect. Even worse, it's possible for students to study history across years 7 to 10 without ever learning about ancient Egypt, Greece and Rome, medieval Europe and epochal events like the renaissance and the Industrial Revolution.

Three of the cross-curricula priorities informing history, in addition to other subjects, are Aboriginal and Torres Strait Islander

Histories and Cultures, Sustainability and Asia and Australia's Engagement with Asia. While there are literally hundreds of references to Indigenous history, culture and spirituality the impact and significance of Western civilisation and Judeo-Christianity is treated in a superficial and fragmented fashion. Christianity is rarely, if ever, mentioned and while the dark side of Western civilisation is emphasised (including slavery, mistreatment of women, the stolen generation, mandatory detention and the civil rights movement both in Australia and America), Indigenous culture and history are presented in a positive light and beyond reproach.

In relation to Asia, and similar to the way Indigenous culture and history is treated, students are presented with a sanitised picture. A picture that ignores and air brushes from history the millions starved, tortured and killed under dictators like Mao, Pol Pot and Ho Chi Minh. Whereas Australia is a Westminster, parliamentary democracy where people's rights and freedoms are protected there is also no mention in the national curriculum that the majority of Asian countries are totalitarian, single party regimes where property can be confiscated, and people imprisoned and denied the rights we take for granted without any protection or recourse.

One of the recommendations of the 2014 national curriculum review I co-chaired argued there should be a greater focus on "the contribution of Western civilisation (and) our Judeo-Christian heritage". In response Michael Kindler in *Curriculum Perspectives* (Vol 35, No 1 April 2015) argues:

Many Australians do not have a Western, so termed "Judeo-Christian heritage". Such a recommendation ignores the multicultural, multi-faith composition of contemporary Australia, and recommends privileging one over another, when a pluralist would recognise that one interpretation of civilisation and its heritage should stand equally and alongside any other.

Cultural relativism and identity politics prevail ignoring the reality Australia's political and legal institutions and much of our language, literature, music and art are inherited from Europe and Ireland and the United Kingdom. While the numbers are diminishing it's also true Christianity is Australia's mainstream religion and the nation's political and legal institutions and way of life are indebted to Christianity.

THE LONG MARCH THROUGH THE UNIVERSITIES

The humourless and relentless policing of language, so as to prevent heretical thoughts from arising, the violence done to traditional categories and natural ways of describing things, the obliterations of memory and assiduous policing of the past – all these things, so disturbingly described in Nineteen Eighty-Four, *are now routinely to be observed on university campuses on both sides of the Atlantic...*

Roger Scruton, *Conservatism*

Universities, as a result of the '60s and '70s cultural revolution and the decision by the cultural-left to take the long march through the institutions, have especially been affected by politically correct ideology and wokeness. Such is the dominance of neo-Marxist and postmodern inspired ideology that left-of-centre academics, especially in sociology, history, cultural studies, English and the law, dominate departments and faculties across the English-speaking world. Research carried out by the American based Heterodox Academy concludes "The data for three campus constituencies unequivocally show that liberals are considerably overrepresented on university and college campuses. And the research on campus climate reveals a decrease in openness to no-liberal viewpoints". The British thinktank the Adam Smith Institute draws a similar conclusion when arguing "Individuals with left-wing and liberal views are overrepresented in British academia. Those with right-wing and conservative views are correspondingly underrepresented. Around 50% of the general public supports right-wing or conservative parties, compared to less than 12% of academics".

Like the school curriculum, historically a university education has centred on a liberal education; one that has its origins in Europe and the United Kingdom and that can be traced back to ancient Greece and philosophers like Aristotle, Socrates and Plato. Such an education as argued by Cardinal Newman in *The Idea of a University* inculcates a particular habit of mind involving "freedom, equitableness, calmness, moderation, and wisdom; or what in a previous discourse I have ventured to call a philosophical habit". As previously noted, the English poet T.S. Eliot in *Notes Towards a Definition of Culture* argues in a similar vein when suggesting universities "should stand for the preservation of learning, for the pursuit of truth, and in so far as men are capable of it, the attainment of wisdom".

A liberal education is not immediately utilitarian or concerned with enforcing a particular ideology or political philosophy. As noted by the American academic, Israel Scheffler, in *Reflections on Educational Relevance*, a balanced, objective and impartial education must be allowed to:

> *... facilitate independent evaluation of social practice... as instruments of insight and criticism, standing apart from current social conceptions and serving autonomous ideals of inquiry and truth.*

Such has been the destructive impact of the cultural-left's

takeover of universities that Pierre Ryckmans, a sinologist who taught at the Australian National University and The University of Sydney, argues the liberal concept of a university no longer exists. In his 1996 Boyer Lectures *The View from the Bridge* Ryckmans describes a young academic attacking a visiting speaker for his "narrow bourgeois elitism" for daring to discuss the importance of Chines literati painting.

In addition to rehashing slogans made popular by Mao's cultural revolution the young academic argues it is impossible to discriminate or be objective as all value judgements are relative and subjective. Ryckman's replies "to deny the existence of objective values is to deprive the university of its spiritual means of operation". Such is his distaste and hostility to what a university education has been reduced to Ryckmans concludes:

> *The main problem is not so much that the University as Western civilization knew it, is now dead, but that its death has hardly registered in the consciousness of the public, and even the majority of academics themselves.*

Ryckmans is not alone in his pessimistic and disturbing summation of the impact of cultural-left ideology and the deleterious impact of critical theory and its more recent progeny.

Merv Bendle, a Senior Lecturer in History and Communication at James Cook University, also criticises the subservience to cultural-left theories and criticises Australian academics for their "simplistic default position of class, sex, race" and for uncritically advocating "politically correct positions which are widely shared and immune to criticism". When detailing what he sees as the unremitting attacks on Western culture caused by "an ideological contagion of shame and self-loathing" ('The Suicide of the West', *Quadrant*, 17 October 2016) Bendle argues this "nihilistic worldview is now institutionalized throughout Western academia". In relation to Australia, Bendle argues this bleak view, drawing on existentialism to deconstructionism, "has been systematically promoted throughout academia, the schools and the media".

John Carroll, formally at La Trobe University, puts a similar case when arguing Australia's cultural elites, including universities, the school curricula, museums and art galleries, no longer are committed to rationality and objectivity exemplified by "the Western tradition since classical Greece". Carroll argues in 'How I became a political conservative' (*Quadrant*, 9 May 2015):

> *The Left impulse has been less calmly quizzical, more aggressively hostile, seeking to undermine existing authorities without replacing them. Accordingly, art has to be shocking; values have to be deconstructed; meanings have to be exposed as rationalisations for entrenched wealth and privilege.*

The British art critic and academic, Giles Auty who settled in Australia, also condemns the cultural-left's takeover of the academy and the pernicious influence of what he describes as postmodernism and political correctness. Auty describes postmodernism as "a deeply anti-democratic political as well as a cultural movement". One that constitutes "leftist totalitarianism by stealth" and that is now rampant in our schools and universities. As a result Auty concludes in 'How the West is Really Being Lost' (*Quadrant* Online, 29 June 2018):

The widespread politicisation of culture and the arts in Australia has had a particularly unfortunate effect on all kinds of aesthetic judgments, which are widely dismissed today as elements of an outdated bourgeois Western culture.

American campuses since the heady days of the late 1960s have also become a victim of the culture wars. As noted by Alan Bloom in *Closing of the American Mind* published in 1987 "The American University in the sixties was experiencing the same dismantling of the structure of rational inquiry as had the German universities in the thirties. No longer believing in their higher vocation, both gave way to a highly ideologized student populace". Subsequent authors including Roger Kimball, Dinesh D'Souza and more recently Helen Pluckrose and James Lindsay have detailed the steady decline of academic impartiality and reason as wokeness became the new orthodoxy stifling any opposition.

What constitutes the purpose of education and a worthwhile curriculum has also been radically redefined in universities in the United Kingdom. Cultural critics including Roger Scruton, Douglas Murray and Frank Furedi detail at some length the nature and impact of the left's long march through the institutions. In *Where Have All The Intellectuals Gone* Furedi warns against the impact of woke, postmodern relativism and subjectivity. A radical perspective that denies knowledge has any intrinsic meaning or value, that there are no truths and that the purpose of education is restricted to what is immediately relevant and utilitarian. The most bizarre example of woke, post-colonial ideology involves the Department of Animal and Plant Sciences at the University of

Sheffield where UK science is condemned as "inherently white". The woke academics believe non-Western science perspectives must be adopted as the European scientific Enlightenment "was both a fundamental contributor to European imperialism and a major beneficiary of its injustices... it's clear that science cannot be objective and apolitical".

RADICAL GENDER AND SEXUALITY THEORY

Since the Frankfurt School championed critical theory to critique and demolish capitalism and to herald the new socialist utopia a rainbow alliance of related theories has entered the culture wars. One of the most influential theories relates to the way once accepted and long held beliefs about gender and sexuality, especially the nuclear family, have been deconstructed and transformed. In an essay titled 'The Ascendance of Eroticism' Del Noce traces the current sexual and gender revolution to Wilhelm Reich's *The Sexual Revolution* published in 1930. Central to Reich's critique of Western societies is the belief capitalism is guilty of imposing what is described as repressive morality. After noting the impact of Reich's book on the cultural revolution of the '60s De Noce writes:

> *... he replaced the categories of bourgeoisie and proletariat with those of the advocates of repressive morality... and the advocates of sexual freedom. Supposedly, only such a replacement and the achievement of sexual happiness would lead to the extinction of the authoritarian spirit and to a form of internationalism free from all compromises.*

Another significant figure responsible for the sexual revolution transforming Western societies, where one's sexual identity is a dynamic and fluid social construct and where marriage is no longer defined as consecrating the union between woman and a man, is Dr John William Money who worked at John Hopkins

University. According to *The Shorter Oxford Dictionary* gender is a grammatical term used to distinguish whether particular words relate to males, females or are neutral. What is revolutionary is the way Money redefined the word gender to refer to the way individuals self-identify regarding their sexuality. Being male, female or anywhere on the LGBTIQ+ spectrum is no longer determined by whether a person was born a girl or a boy. Money also pioneered research into the nature and impact of gender dysphoria and was one of the first medical practitioners to recommend sex reassignment surgery.

As previously mentioned, one of the most egregious examples of gender theory is the Australian Safe Schools program championed by Roz Ward when she was an academic at La Trobe University in the Australian Research Centre in Sex, Health and Society. Ward has made no secret of her conviction that promoting a radical gender and sexuality theory on school children is one way to bring about a new world order of sexual liberation and freedom. As previously quoted, Ward argues "It will only be through a revitalised class struggle and revolutionary change that we can hope for the liberation of LGBTIQ+ people."

Central to this battle is redefining gender and sexuality as social constructs instead of a biological imperative and a scientific fact. The material endorsed by the Safe Schools Coalition argues that gender and sexuality are fluid concepts and criticises heterosexism as a binary, oppressive concept. Students as young as eight and 10 are told to celebrate diversity and difference on the basis "there are many genders beyond 'male' or 'female'; gender can be fluid or limitless" and that "There are no rules about who you can be: all you need to do is be yourself". The definition of being LGBTIQ+ is based on self-identification and has nothing to do with one's sex at birth or what the Bible says about God creating Adam and Eve.

The bias evident in the Safe Schools Coalition program is further illustrated by its claim that the program is justified because 15.7% of students are either same sex attracted, gender diverse, trans or intersex ("Stand Out" – Safe Schools Coalition). Ignored is the research demonstrating that heterosexuality is the norm and that while LGBTIQ+ people should never be unfairly discriminated against they are a small minority of the population.

Research carried out by Anthony Smith and Paul Badcock from Victoria's La Trobe University conclude approximately 98 per cent of men and women aged 16–59 identify as heterosexual. In the survey only 1.6 per cent of men identify as gay and 0.9 as bisexual while 0.8 of women describe themselves as lesbian and 1.4 as bisexual. In a paper published in *People and Place* Vol 12, No 4, 2004, Shaun Wilson writes:

> *This paper confirms earlier research estimating the GBLT population at around two per cent of the Australian adult population with higher numbers of gay and bisexual men than lesbian and bisexual women.*

Professor Patrick Parkinson from the University of Sydney also concludes the overwhelming majority of the population in Australia and the United Sates is heterosexual. He writes "Large scale surveys in recent years (when homosexual orientation has become normalised and therefore much less likely to be a matter which people fail to disclose) put the figures on same-sex attraction in the adult population as between 1% to 3%".

Also ignored is the research showing, notwithstanding that puberty and adolescence are a time of experimentation and anxiety about gender and sexuality (thus suggesting the behaviour might be more widespread), that by the time adolescents pass through puberty and reach adulthood many are happy to be females or males.

The La Trobe University's Australian Research Centre in Sex, Health and Society is one of the principal supporters of the Safe Schools Coalition and is responsible for a resource titled *The Practical Guide to Love, Sex and Relationships.* Like the Safe Schools Program the material advocates a strong LGBTIQ+ agenda that argues society is guilty of enforcing a Eurocentric and heteronormative view of gender; one that impacts negatively on boys and girls.

One of the activities titled "Freedom Fighters" asks students to role play a situation where Martians invade and enforce a destructive binary code – where boys are boys and girls are girls. Students are then asked to be freedom fighters where the "male" hero sings:

> You don't have to be a certain way just because you have a penis
> You don't have to be a certain way just because you have a vagina
> We're not gonna care about that
> We're gonna do what we wanna do

We're gonna be who we wanna be
I'm gonna lead you guys to victory and then I'm gonna go home and enjoy my collection of vintage dolls
Because we're free, damn it
And they may take our penises
They may take our vaginas
But they will never take our freedom!

NEO-MARXIST CRITICAL THEORY AND THE IMPACT OF CULTURAL MARXISM

Although most au courant disciples think of themselves as progressive activists, or at least on the progressive side of history, their philosophy releases relativist and nihilist forces that culminate in coercive ideologies. This the paradox of the relativist authoritarian.

Dinesh D'Souza, *Illiberal Education*

As highlighted in George Orwell's novel *1984*, language and how it is used significantly influences how we think and act and controlling language is a key strategy employed by totalitarian regimes of the left and the right to manipulate people and enforce group think. In Orwell's dystopian novel what is described as Newspeak leads to a situation where "thoughtcrime" is impossible as "there will be no words in which to express it".

Such is the insidious evil of distorting language to control how people think Orwell writes in "Looking back on the Spanish Civil War", we now live in a world:

> *... in which the Leader, or some ruling clique, controls not only the future but the past ... If he says that two and two are five – well, two and two are five. This prospect frightens me much more than bombs.*

The slogan employed during Australia's same-sex marriage debate "Love is Love" is also an example of politically correct language use. Taken on face value such a statement appears reasonable and beyond dispute – all should be free to love whoever they choose and the State who no right to decide otherwise. A closer reflection, though, suggests that not all types of love are the same or they should be treated equally. The love between a woman and a man that culminates in marriage and the possibility of procreation is heterosexual in nature and throughout history and in most cultures is considered preeminent. The love between a man and a man or a woman and a woman is clearly not the same type of love. Similarly, the love a parent has for a child or the type of love between siblings is also very different to the love between a wife and a husband.

While the cultural-left's use of politically correct language is widespread and now dominates public and private discourse it should be noted that using language to persuade and convince has been evident since the time of the ancient Greek philosophers and sophists. What is called rhetoric, both verbal and written, includes devices such as:

- using emotive language,
- attacking the person,
- appealing to expert opinion and facts,
- generalising from one or two examples,
- employing logic and reason and
- basing one's argument on personal experience.

It also should be noted that employing rhetoric is not restricted to the cultural-left. During America's involvement in the Vietnam war the military used the expression "collateral damage" to describe innocent civilians being injured or killed and "friendly fire" when its soldiers were the victims of American firepower. Forcefully removing peasants from their farms and villages, instead of being described for what it was, was labelled as "pacification".

Notwithstanding rhetoric is common across the political spectrum what distinguishes political correctness and wokeness from other forms of argument and language use is that:

- it is primarily used as a strategy by the cultural-left,
- while originating as an off shoot of classical Marxism it has since morphed into a rainbow alliance of cultural-left theories including: cultural Marxism, feminism, postmodernism, deconstruction and LGBTQI+, post-colonial and gender and sexuality theories,
- Western civilisation, capitalism and the free market, Judeo-Christianity, marriage between a woman and a man and heterosexuality are its chief enemies,
- identity politics and victimhood prevail where so-called disadvantaged individuals and groups, such as women, LGBTIQ+ and Indigenous people and those of colour and non-European ethnicity and culture, are always presented as victims made powerless by an oppressive system,
- rather than relying on reason and rationality (as such concepts are Eurocentric, phallocentric and binary) arguments are subjective and relative in nature and based on emotion, and

- the intention is to challenge what is condemned as the status quo and to impose a new-age, politically correct utopia where diversity and difference reign supreme, all are equal and free of discrimination (unless you are a white, male, older, Eurocentric male) and individuals are empowered and no longer constrained by the past and the obsolete institutions associated with Western civilisation.

As noted by Jennifer Oriel in *Cancel Culture and the Left's Long March*, an even more insidious and dangerous aspect of woke language control and group think is any opposition or criticism is vilified and attacked without remorse. Civil debate and reasoned dialogue have given way to personal attacks and vitriol. Examples of those attacked and punished include Australia's Christian rugby union player Israel Folau for condemning homosexuality, James Cook University's Peter Ridd for questioning the impact of global warming on the Great Barrier Reef, J.K. Rowling and Germaine Greer for questioning transgenderism and the head of the British soccer chairman Greg Clarke resigning for using politically incorrect language.

Oriel traces the climate of intolerance and vilification and the abandonment of impartial and balanced debate to Herbert Marcuse's essay 'Repressive Tolerance' when she writes:

> *In 1965, Marcuse justified the new form of inequality that would be made manifest by censoring right-of-centre freethinkers. In* Repressive Tolerance *he wrote "The conclusion reached is that the realization of the objective of tolerance would call for intolerance toward prevailing attitudes, opinions, and*

the extension of tolerance to policies, attitudes and opinions which are outlawed or suppressed... what is proclaimed and practiced as tolerance today, is in many of its most effective manifestations serving the cause of oppression".

Recent events involving Australia's universities illustrate the success of the cultural-left's political correctness movement in influencing and controlling how people communicate, think and interact with one another. In the language of *1984*'s Big Brother the University of Sydney proudly proclaims the purpose of education is to "unlearn". On the basis "not everyone has been taught how to unlearn" the university exhorts students to "challenge the established, demolish social norms" in areas such as same-sex marriage, indigenous land rights, peace studies, refugees and the environment.

Victoria's Monash University, the University of New South Wales and South Australia's Flinders University have Diversity Toolkits and Inclusivity Guidelines that tell academics and students what to say and what to think instead of promoting open discussion and dialogue. Academics are told what they teach:

- should celebrate diversity and difference,
- be careful not to espouse "heteronormativity" and "heterosexism",
- that Australia was "invaded" and that it's wrong to say Captain Cook discovered what is now Australia or that at the time indigenous peoples were "primitive" or "native" compared to Europeans,
- academics are also warned about misguided students

"who see themselves as part of the dominant culture" and who might react against being told all cultures are equal and worthy of respect.

Ignored, unlike Aboriginal and Torres Strait Islander cultures, is Western civilisation at the time of the First Fleet was characterised by:

- complex forms of irrigation, husbandry and agriculture,
- the printing press,
- advanced political and legal systems,
- cities that housed thousands,
- explorers and navigators who had circumnavigated the globe and
- the adoption of technology and science that led to steam engines, telescopes, microscopes and the rudimentary beginnings of modern sanitation, hygiene and medicine.

And while there is no doubt that Western civilisation drew on and made use of discoveries and scientific innovations taken from Chinese and Islamic cultures the reality is that it is only in the West civilisation achieved so much in terms of material, scientific, technological and social progress.

Monash University's 'Inclusive Language Guide' provides another example of how advocates of political correctness have taken the long march through the institutions. On the basis that "language is enormously powerful and politically charged" the guide suggests using "workforce" instead of "manpower" and "artificial" instead of "manmade".

Australian universities also have Safe Spaces where Muslim,

women, LGBTIQ+ and Indigenous students are guaranteed a secure and safe environment free from supposedly hostile white, Eurocentric, heteronormative and racist students. As three Queensland white students found out when they entered a computer centre reserved for indigenous students and subsequently complained about their treatment on social networking site retribution soon follows those who transgress.

In addition to having to spend thousands of dollars defending themselves against a complaint of being racist bought under section 18c of the Racial Discrimination Act the students also faced being publicly criticised for simply expressing a valid point of view.

Trigger warnings are also increasingly prevalent where vulnerable students are warned beforehand if they are about to encounter supposedly offensive or challenging texts or other material. Examples include literature that deals with homosexuality, violence, rape, death, racism or mental illness. Taken to its conclusion literary texts such as *Macbeth* (violence and murder), the play *Medea* (where children are killed) and novels like *The Man Who Loved Children* (where someone commits suicide) are decidedly problematic and offensive.

Governments, local councils and companies like Australia's airline Qantas are also involved in promoting PC language. The Victorian government's inclusive language guide criticises the relationship between men and women on the basis "Heteronormativity is the assumption that everyone is heterosexual (straight), and that this is the norm" and "heterosexism is the belief that non-heteronormative sexual orientations or gender identities are unnatural".

As previously stated, the fact that approximately 98 per cent of Australians self-identify as male or female and that the natural order of things is for men and women to procreate to ensure the survival of humanity is ignored. Also ignored, as doctors and nurses well know, is that the physiology of the human body is better suited to a heterosexual relationship.

How literature is taught at Sydney University also adopts a decidedly postmodern, politically correct approach. Instead of the Western culture's literary canon, students learn about "the rise of identity politics, the culture wars and queer theory". Under the heading "postcolonial modernisms/modernities" students learn how "race, gender, class, sexuality, nation and religion shape ideas of being modern".

If classic texts such as Shakespeare's tragedies are studied, students are made to deconstruct them in terms of power relationships involving the new trinity of gender, ethnicity and class. A third subject involves deconstructing "text-production as a social and ideological act", where students consider the "ideological influences impacting on theoretical discourse about language and textuality".

This politically correct view of literature is the opposite to that associated with a liberal view of education; one where literature is studied for its moral and aesthetic significance and value. Instead of appreciating how language is employed and crafted or what a literary work suggests about what it means to be human and how we relate to the others and the wider world the focus is on deconstructing texts in terms of critical theory.

Universities in the United Kingdom have also succumbed to

the Kool-Aid. Manchester University, for example, in its "Guide to inclusive language" descriptions like man, woman, father, mother are replaced by individuals and guardians. Other words now excluded include man-made, manpower and mankind. The Brighton and Sussex University's Hospitals NHS Trust now tells midwifes to replace breastmilk with human milk or chest milk, breast feeding with chest feeding and father with second biological father.

Such is the power of Orwellian language control that even the United States Congress is no longer immune. In early 2021 the Rules Package, released by Nancy Pelosi and James P. McGovern both Democrats, is described as the most "inclusive in history" with specific mention of honouring "all gender identities by changing pronouns and familial relationships in the House rules to be gender neutral". Examples include replacing seaman with sea farers, Chairman with Chair and replacing he or she serves with such Member, Delegate or Resident Commissioner serves. An even more extreme example of politically correct, woke language is clause 8 (c) (3) where descriptions including father, mother, son, daughter, brother, sister, uncle, aunt, husband, wife are cancelled as considered somehow offensive to LGBTIQ+ activists.

WHAT'S TO BE DONE?

The first step in countering the destructive and poisonous influence of political correctness and wokeness is to call it out and reveal its true nature. While disguised as the need to be courteous and polite and not unfairly criticise others both are virulent and oppressive forms of thought control and group think. Whether by corrupting language or enforcing cultural-left ideology on issues like gender and sexuality, immigration, multiculturalism, Judeo-Christianity or the significance of Western civilisation the purpose is to radically reshape society.

Underlying political correctness is the impact of critical theory that can be traced back to the cultural revolution of the late 1960s and before then the establishment of the Frankfurt School in Germany in the 1920s. The impact of postmodernism has also been instrumental in denying rationality and reason and imposing a nihilistic view of knowledge where power, drawing primarily on Foucault, is the defining characteristic. Realising there was no chance of a revolution in the West, as had occurred in Russia under Lenin, neo-Marxist academics argued the way to success was to take the long march through the institutions. Best illustrated by Roger Kimball's quotation previously referred to, the focus is on capturing and radically transforming society by targeting institutions like schools, universities, churches, intermediary organisations and the media.

The cultural-left is also able to achieve its goals by arguing any change is minor and incremental in nature, thus, disguising the often radical and extreme nature of what is intended. Same sex marriage, when first championed by the cultural-left, simply involved changing the definition to include gays and lesbians but it now encompasses the full range of LGBTIQ+ people as well as initiating a wider campaign to normalise radical gender and sexuality theories in the school curriculum. Faith-based schools, in particular, are now being pressured to adopt staffing and enrolment policies running counter to the religious beliefs such schools are called upon to uphold.

The second step is to learn from the success of the cultural-left and to adapt its strategies where relevant and useful. Adopting a medium to long term view is critical as is the need to formulate well defined strategies, including engaging in the battle of ideas in the public arena as well as universities, schools, the workplace and in one's private life. One of the defining differences between the cultural-left and those more conservative is the Left's ability to appoint advocates and fellow travellers to key positions in professional bodies, unions, educational organisations and tertiary institutions.

In relation to education in Australia it's no secret that those imbued with cultural-left ideology and group think either gain or are appointed to senior and influential positions across key organisations, including: the Australian Curriculum Assessment and Reporting Authority, the Australian Curriculum Studies Association, the Australian Education Union, the Deans of Education and many of the state and territory equivalent bodies. Similar to the old industrial relations club, the way educational policy in areas like the national curriculum is developed involves a small coterie of like-minded individuals all intent on maximising their influence. For many years education in Australia has been the victim of what the New South Wales academic Ken Gannicott describes as provider capture. To say silent is to acquiesce and to vacate the field is to allow the cultural-left to dominate and win control.

The third step is to mobilise and organise like-minded individuals and organisations who are aware of the dangers of the political correctness movement and who are willing and able to join the public battle of ideas. In America groups of like-minded academics opposed to political correctness like the Heterodox Academy and the National Association of Scholars provide a lightning rod for those opposed to cultural-left ideology and a vehicle to express both opposition and what needs to be championed. Individual academics, proven by the success of Canada's Jordan Peterson, America's Helen Pluckrose and James Lindsay plus the UK's Douglas Murray and Roger Scruton, also have a role to play in turning back the woke tide.

Reasserting the primacy of reason, rationality and logic and highlighting the irrational and dangerous nature of political correctness represents the fourth step. To suggest all cultures are equal is to adopt a relativistic position where it is impossible to argue practices like female genital mutilation and child brides are unacceptable. The reality is that Western culture, with its commitment to liberty, freedom and the inherent dignity of the person, is superior to uncivilised, tribal cultures where inequality, injustice and violence are widespread. One of the key reasons so many millions of refugees risk their lives to reach Europe, the United Kingdom, Australia and the United States of America is because they seek the prosperity and liberty denied in their own lands.

The argument that words have no agreed meaning, that knowledge is a social construct based on power relationships and that there are no truths leads to either silence, epistemological suicide or adjudicating truth claims by resorting to violence. As argued by Michael Casey from the Australian Catholic University's PM Glynn Institute in his book *Meaninglessness*:

> *If everything – language, morality, custom, culture, and human life itself – is nothing more than what it is described to be from time to time, then everything is subordinate to and forever in the service of power, to be made and remade at whim.*

Such is the extreme and bizarre nature of the woke movement it is also vital to be able to laugh and to reveal that the emperor has no clothes. Humour and satire are key weapons against the thought-police intent on stifling debate and enforcing sterile group think. Arguing it is politically incorrect to order a short black coffee as it might offend people of colour or that Santa Claus can no longer say "Ho, Ho, Ho" because it might be mistaken for the American slang for a prostitute is ridiculous. Anyone who has read Swift's *A Modest Proposal* detailing how to solve the Irish problem during the famine or his description of the Academy of Lagado in *Gulliver's Travels* will appreciate the power of satire in calling out cant, hypocrisy and group think.

POSTSCRIPT

One of the defining features of any civilised society is the ability to think rationally and logically and to be able to debate and discuss often controversial and contentious issues in an objective and impartial manner. A second defining feature is the need to ensure each succeeding generation is initiated into the culture in which they are born and where they will be future citizens; described as enculturation. As a result of political correctness, both features are attacked and undermined – leading to cultural amnesia and eventual suicide.

The reality that cultural-left ideology is so widespread and influential should not disguise the fact there is opposition and cause for optimism. Human nature is such that the thirst for liberty and freedom and the need to find a more spiritual and transcendent sense of self and the purpose of life can never be fully extinguished. It's also true, notwithstanding its flaws and sins, Western civilisation underpinned by the search for knowledge, beauty, wisdom and truth has much to acknowledge and defend. Illustrated by the television series *The Ascent of Man* presented by Jacob Bronowski, over a period of thousands of years Western civilisation's discoveries and accomplishments have led to the printing press, the steam engine, electricity, modern medicine and hygiene, digital technology, splitting the atom and putting a man on the moon and increasing food production and the standard of living tenfold.

It is also true, as argued by Kenneth Clark in another television series titled *Civilisation*, the West's heritage of art, music, literature, dance and architecture provides an evocative, rich and fulfilling legacy without which life would be barren, sterile and without purpose. While other civilisations have their unique way of expressing and exploring existential questions about the purpose of life and the nature of the world in which we live it is Western culture that is in many ways preeminent. It is Western civilisation that is responsible for the *Iliad* and the *Odyssey* and authors including Sophocles, Euripides, Shakespeare, William Blake, Austen, Yeats, Chekhov, Ibsen, Dostoyevsky, T.S. Eliot, Sylvia Plath, James Joyce and Patrick White (to name a few). Add composers like Bach, Mozart, Chopin, Faure, Beethoven, Vivaldi and Tchaikovsky and artists including Michelangelo, Rubens, Rembrandt, Van Gough, Matisse, Monet and Monat and it is soon apparent there is much to acknowledge and celebrate.

The West's political and legal systems, drawing on the New Testament and liberalism, is also unique and worth defending against those intent on imposing totalitarian language control and group think. Documents like *Magna Carta*, Tom Paine's *The Rights of Man* and Mary Wollstonecraft's *A Vindication of the Rights of Woman*, the American *Declaration of Independence* and the United Nation's *Universal Declaration of Human Rights*, once again, are uniquely Western in origin. Such rights do not exist in primitive, tribal cultures characterised by superstition and witchcraft or totalitarian dictatorships where violence and intimidation ensure compliance.

ABOUT THE AUTHOR

Since first warning about the dangers of political correctness during the mid-1990s Dr Kevin Donnelly has established a reputation as one of Australia's leading conservative commentators and authors fighting against politically correct group think and language control that are undermining Western societies and stifling free and open debate.

In 2016 Kevin was made a Member of the Order of Australia for services to education and he is currently a Senior Fellow at the Australian Catholic University's PM Glynn Institute. Kevin's website is kevindonnelly.com.au and he can be contacted at kevind@netspace.net.au

He is the author of *How Political Correctness is Destroying Australia*, *How Political Correctness is Destroying Education*, *How Political Correctness is Still Destroying Australia*, *Christianity is Good For Us*, and is the editor of *Cancel Culture and the Left's Long March* and *Christianity Matters*.